Bouldering
Rocky Mountain National Park & Mount Evans

Jamie Emerson

Sharp End Publishing
Authentic Guides From Core Climbers

Bouldering Rocky Mountain National Park & Mt. Evans BY JAMIE EMERSON

Published and distributed by
Sharp End Publishing, LLC
PO Box 1613
Boulder, CO 80306
t. 303.444.2698
www.sharpendbooks.com

ISBN: 978-1-892540-72-0
Library of Congress Control Number: 2011929856
Printed in Korea

Cover Photo Credit
Carlo Traversi on Sunseeker V13. Photo by Andy Mann.

Opening Page Photo Credit
Angela Payne on The Automator V13. Photo by John Dickey.

Unlabeled Photo Credit
Jamie Emerson, Wade David

Table of Contents Photo Credit
Tyler Landman on Ode to the Modern Man V14. Photo by Wade David

READ THIS BEFORE USING THIS GUIDE

Rock climbing, including bouldering, is extremely dangerous. A small and incomplete list of possible dangers include: loose rock, bad landings (eg. landing on uneven or rocky terrain, landing on a spotter). Unlike roped climbing, every bouldering fall is a ground fall. As a result, the boulderer risks serious injury or death with every attempt. Falls are common while bouldering.

The symbols used in this guide describe boulders with almost certain injury potential. It is, however, highly probable that you could seriously injure yourself on a problem that doesn't receive a highball or bad landing designation.

THE AUTHOR AND PUBLISHER EXPRESSLY DISCLAIM ALL REPRESENTATIONS AND WARRANTIES REGARDING THIS GUIDE, THE ACCURACY OF THE INFORMATION CONTAINED HEREIN, AND THE RESULTS OF YOUR USE HEREOF, INCLUDING WITHOUT LIMITATION, IMPLIED WARRANTIES OR MERCHANTABILITY AND FITNESS FOR A PARTICULAR PURPOSE. THE USER ASSUMES ALL RISK ASSOCIATED WITH THE USE OF THIS GUIDE.

It is your responsibility to take care of yourself while bouldering. Seek a professional instructor or guide if you are unsure of your ability to handle any circumstances that may arise. This guide is not intended as an instructional manual.

Acknowledgments:

I would like to extend a tremendous thank you to each and every person who has helped in the making of this guidebook. It is the product of 10 years of bouldering in the mountains of Colorado, and it would be nothing without the help of many of my friends, my family and everyone out there who shares in the game we play.

A special thanks goes out to: Five Ten, Organic Crashpads, E-Grips, Brian Capps, Bennett Scott, Angela Payne, Ryan Olson, Justin Jaeger, David Graham, Chad Greedy, Tiffany Hensley, Jason Pinto, Caroline Treadway, Dave Ludders, Jon Cardwell, Stephanie Marvez, Flannery Shay-Nemirow, Phil Schaal, Hayden Miller, Rylan Marshall, Tommy Caldwell, Daniel Woods, Andre DiFelice, and Brian Camp for their knowledge, sense of humor, motivation, devotion to the sport and help with this guidebook. This guidebook would not have been possible without the love and support of my parents Collin and Shawn Emerson and my brother, Brady.

Other boulderers and friends I would like to thank are:

Ryan Anglemeyer
Samuel Beckett
Tom Blackford
Bruce Bright
Mike Brooks
Mike Caldwell
Albert Camus
Rob Candelaria
George Capps
Chris Craft
Cameron Cross
Paul Dusatko
Herm Feissner
Chuck Fryberger
John Gill
Jon Glassberg
Christian Griffith
Wolfgang Gullich
Naomi Guy
Josh Helke
Adam Henry
Collin Horvat
Nalle Hukkataival
Donell Humphrey
Paul Hunter
Jim Hurst
Ronnie Jenkins
Glenn Johnson
Heather Johnson
Harju Jones
James Joyce
Franz Kafka
Noah Kaufman
Ken Kenny
Jon Linhart
James Litz
Greg Loomis
Steve Mammen
Sarah Marvez
Kelly McBride
Cormac McCarthy
Bronson McDonald
Herman Melville
Theo Merrin
Anne-Worley Moelter
Mike Moelter
Ben Moon
James O'Connor
Nic Oklobzija
Paul Otis
Luke Parady
Sander Pick
Rob Pizem
Alex Puccio
Ayn Rand
Mike Rathke
Paul Robinson
Grandma Schwyn
Ben Scott
Ryan Sewell
Chris Sharma
Asher Shay-Nemirow
John Sherman
Nic Sherman
Ryan Silven
Zack Smith
Adam Strong
Melissa Strong
Gabor Szekely
Jason Tarry
Darin Thompson
Carlo Traversi
Mike Tucker
Jorge Visser
Dave Wahl
Jimmy Webb
Amanda Woods
Steve Woods
Ryan Young

Memories of his home kept recurring and filled his mind. There, too, a church stood in the market-place, partly surrounded by an old graveyard which was again surrounded by a high wall. Very few boys had managed to climb that wall, and for some time K., too, had failed. It was not curiosity which had urged them on. The graveyard had no mystery to them. They had often entered it through a small wicket-gate, it was only the smooth high wall that they had wanted to conquer. But one morning — the empty, quiet marketplace had been flooded with sunshine; when had K. ever seen it like that before or since? — he had succeeded in climbing it with astonishing ease; at a place where he had already slipped down many a time he had clambered with a small flag between his teeth right to the top at the first attempt. Stones were rattling down under his feet, but he was at the top. He stuck the flag in, it flew in the wind, he looked down and round about him, over his shoulder, too, at the crosses mouldering in the ground, nobody was greater than he at that place and that moment.

-Franz Kafka "The Castle"

TABLE OF CONTENTS

Longs Peak and Lake Haiyaha Photo: Caroline Treadway

For many climbers, bouldering in the Mt. Evans Wilderness Area and Rocky Mountain National Park represents a near-perfect experience. The towering peaks, unpredictable weather, rocky landings, difficult problems, long days and breathtaking scenery all combine for a unique adventure found nowhere else in the world.

Over the past 10 years there has been an explosion of new bouldering in the alpine realms of Colorado. Following this explosion, these areas have become world famous. They are where many of the best boulderers in the country come to test their skill. Of course, along with all of these extreme testpieces are wonderful moderates, and as anyone who has spent time at these fabulous places can attest, it is not so much a place to tick that big number but a place to be humbled — and a place to be inspired.

Perhaps it is fitting that some of the most extreme problems in the country, in terms of difficulty, approaches and landings, are found in some of the most extreme terrain in the country. The complex nature of the topography in the mountains presents some very interesting challenges for a guidebook author. I have spent thousands of hours hiking the hills, studying the terrain, and learning the subtleties of the land. I have committed myself to understanding the complex setting and the often hidden locations of the hundreds of problems tucked away in the chaotic corners of these dark cathedrals.

I first visited the Park in the fall of 2001 and was enamored with the rock, the style, and the setting. Over the course of the last 10 years, I have spent more than 400 days bouldering in RMNP alone. During that time I also began climbing at Mt. Evans and my love for bouldering in the wilderness was born. It was also during this time that I began mentally recording all that had been done over the years.

I was approached by several members of the community to take the lead and assemble all of this information. It has been a labor of love for me personally, and for many who have helped out along the way. I have talked to and included as many people in the Front Range climbing community as possible. I have done everything I can to make this a book by the community and for the community. I know these areas as well as anywhere and to love something is to know it. I am fortunate enough to be able to share that knowledge with you.

-Jamie Emerson, summer 2011

Lay of the Land Area Overview

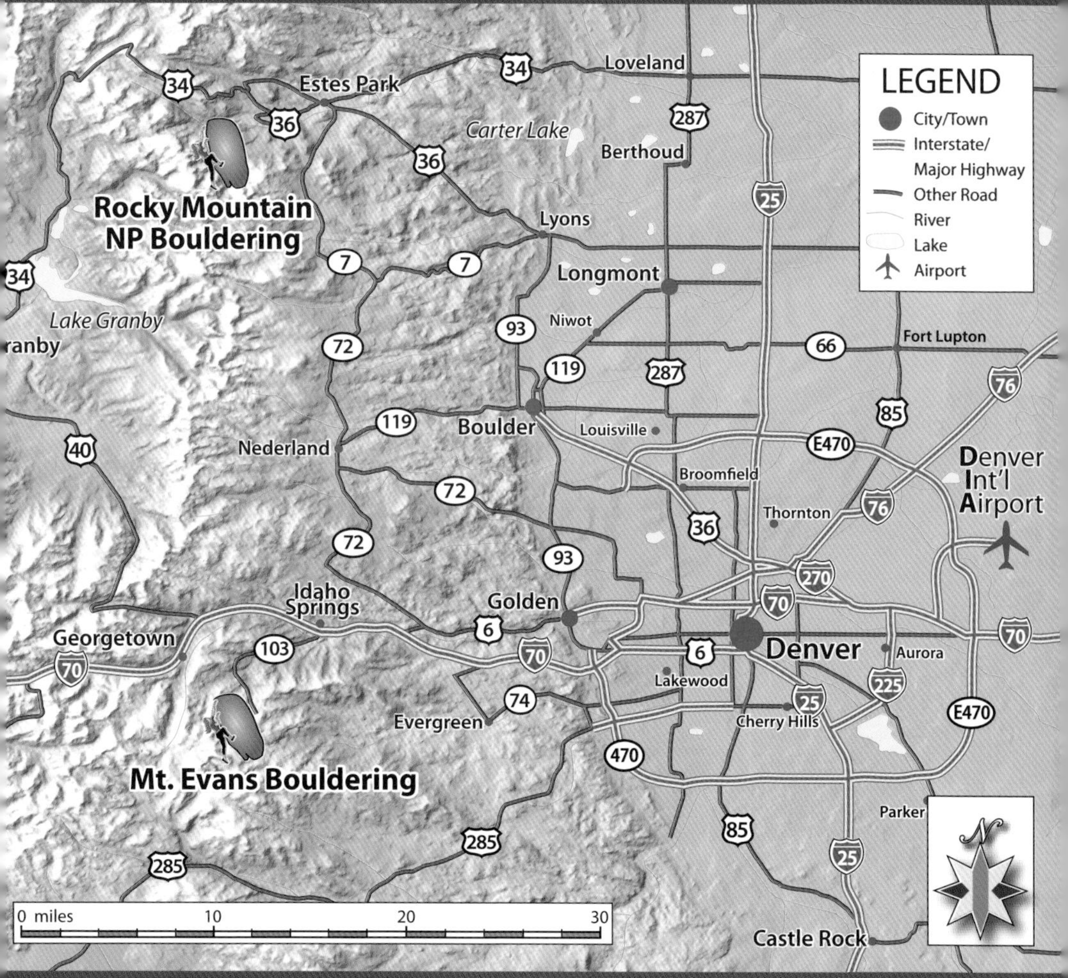

Indian Paintbrush blossoms near the shore of Emerald Lake, RMNP

Guidebook Features:

Areas

This guidebook covers the bouldering in the Mt. Evans Wilderness (Area A and Area B) near Idaho Springs, Colorado, as well as Rocky Mountain National Park (RMNP), just outside Estes Park, Colorado. Areas in RMNP include Moraine Park, Veritas, Stinkbug, Emerald Lake, the Hallett Boulder, and Lower and Upper Chaos Canyon (near Lake Haiyaha). Several areas at Mt. Evans and in RMNP have been omitted at the request of the rangers.

Area / Problem Names

Most of the areas described in this book have been developed in the last 10 years. Whenever possible, the name used is the name assigned by the first ascentionist for a problem. Some problems are known by two names and when the information was available both names are included. If a problem was not previously named, I occasionally came up with a new name. Otherwise it is simply left as the grade with no name. There are several somewhat offensive names listed, and they have not been changed in an attempt to be historically accurate.

Area / Problem Descriptions

In addition to written directions, there are also maps and photographs to almost all of the areas. The mountains present a difficult and unique challenge in directing climbers to where they want to go. In reading the written descriptions, looking at the photos, and studying the maps, there should be enough information to get you to the problems you want to see.

In America, the ethic for repeating a problem is to start on the same holds as the first ascentionist. Most of the problems described in the guidebook have specific starting holds. If it makes a significant difference whether to sit, squat or stand, the pertinent information is included so the guidebook user can make a proper repeat. The mountains are filled with literally thousands of boulders and rock faces. This guide does not attempt to get the reader to every one of these faces, sometimes because of access issues, sometimes in an effort to preserve some level of adventure. Directions are given to the most worthwhile problems.

The Star System

In 2001, Brian Capps and Matt Wilder scoped an amazing project in Squamish, BC at the base of the Grand Wall, known locally as "The Room Project." They felt this line had all the attributes of a classic problem: an obvious starting hold, excellent rock, a flat landing, and an obvious and uncontrived line. In an attempt to standardize and objectify its quality, they created their own bouldering star system. Most guidebooks use some sort of quality rating, but the system developed by Capps and Wilder was intended to be used across the country. Their original justification for creating the system was to objectively describe to Fred Nicole, the great Swiss bouldering legend, how good this project was, and this would motivate him to come and climb the line.

The star system used in this book is the system described above, explained to me by Brian Capps. It attempts to objectively rate problems based on several criteria. It should be understood that this system can be applied to any problem in the world. The most important factors would be: the quality of the rock, the purity of the line, the flatness of the landing, the sharpness of the holds, the historical significance of the problem, the setting and the obviousness of the start. This is a similar system used by Matt Wilder in his bouldering guide "Hueco Tanks." However, I have been more strict. The scale described as such would leave room for around 100 problems in the US to be given 4 stars. The 5-star problem is theoretical, as there are still millions of unfound and unclimbed boulders in the world. There are a several 4-star problems described in this guidebook, which would make these problems some of the best in the world. It is important to note that many problems in this guidebook which receive one –or no stars can still be very worthwhile. Fun is subjective, and the scale does not attempt to take away anyone's ability to have fun on a climb that others deem unworthy. It should go without saying that nothing is more fun than long days in the mountains with good friends, falling and flailing on amazing problems, peppered with heated debates about the number of stars those problems should receive!

No stars	Dirty or not especially interesting.
★	This problem possibly has one of the criteria which makes it classic.
★★	This problem may lack several critieria which would make it classic.
★★★	This problem is possibly one of the best in CO, but it lacks at least one key criteria.
★★★★	One of America's best.

Grades

The grading scale used for problems is the Vermin Scale (V Scale). A comparison chart is included to better assist those boulderers who are stuck in the B Scale or in love with the Fountainebleau Scale. There are no slash-grades in the guidebook; however I have acknowledged that some problems are low or high in the grade. Typically, when slash-grades are suggested, there is little incentive for someone to take the lower of the two grades.

I talked to as many local climbers as I could during the preparation of this book, and have thoroughly consulted the internet to give the best possible consensus on grades. If you feel a problem has been overgraded, enjoy the extra points you think you've earned. If you feel like it is sandbagged, make sure not to skip out on that winter campus board session next year. Grades are subjective. The point of even listing them here is to get climbers to things they might be able to climb and enjoy.

Bouldering Grade Chart:

VERMIN	GILL	FONTAINEBLEAU
V0	B1-	
V1	B1	5C
V2	B1	
V3	B1	6A
V4	B1+	6B
V5	B1+	6C/6C+
V6	B2-	7A
V7	B2	7A+/7B
V8	B2	7B+
V9	B2+	7C
V10	B2+	7C+
V11	B2+	8A
V12	B2+	8A+
V13	B2+	8B
V14	B2+	8B+
V15	B2+	8C

Grade Color-Coding

The grades in this guide have been color-coded to help one quickly glance through the book and determine if an area has suitable problems. Thanks to Dave Pegg at Wolverine Publishing for allowing us to use the same scale as Wolverine's Hueco and Bishop books. This can only help climbers who are familiar with Wolverine's fine products.

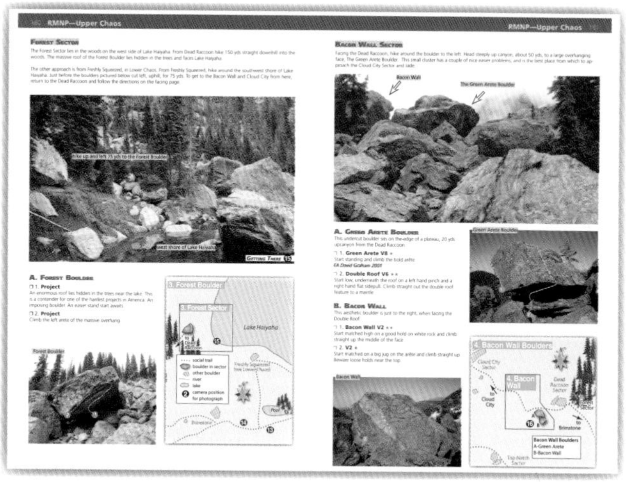

Measurements

Distances and heights are given in either yards or feet. I have gone to great lengths to be as specific as possible when describing problems as accurately as possible. I did not measure each distance with a measuring tool, however, and they are my best estimates. Typically, yards can be equated to long footsteps.

Maps & Photos

The maps in this guide are indespensible in finding the problems, especially when used in conjunction with the text and the photos. Aerial photos were used to trace the locations of the boulders, making the maps virtually to scale. The boulders could often be seen in the photos and great care was taken to draw over the problems themselves. This also ensures that the scale in these maps is as accurate as reasonably possible.

In the beginning of most sections are a series of photographs showing the approaches. In the bottom right corner is a black circle with a white number. Corresponding black circles also appear on the maps. Each area is its own set, beginning at 1. This is a great way for determining your position in the woods. Each area is also broken down into sectors, for ease of description. The sectors are divided by black boxes on the map. In the upper lefthand corner of each sector is a small blue box with a number. This number corresponds to a particular sector, labeled in the key of the map. Navigating this complex mountain territory can be challenging.

WEATHER

Bouldering in the Wilderness

Bouldering in the mountains is a serious endeavor. The extreme nature of the climbing demands a word about what it means to head into the mountains for a day of climbing.

Altitude: The elevation alone can have a very negative effect on those who are not acclimatized. If you are coming from sea level, plan on a few days of hiking to warm up to the steep terrain. It is often surprising how breathless the thin air can leave even seasoned and fit athletes. Those not acclimatized may feel dizziness, shortness of breath, headaches and general nausea. It is not uncommon for climbers from low elevations to become very nauseous and vomit on their first day. It is imperative to bring plenty of food and water. Staying properly fed and hydrated can go a long way to help ward off altitude sickness. The best course of action to help someone who is sick is to get them back down to town as soon as possible; Estes Park and Idaho Springs are both 3,000–4,000 ft below the bouldering areas. It can be assumed that the temperature will drop 3–5 degrees for every 1,000 ft gain in elevation. This means that it can be sunny and 80° F in places like Boulder (5,430 ft) or Denver (5,280 ft), a pleasant 70° F in Estes Park, but it may be a cold and windy 50° F in the upper reaches of the boulderfield.

Talus-hopping Hazards: Navigating the rocky terrain is tricky at best. Some of the most precarious-looking boulders are as solid as can be, and some of the most solid-looking boulders will shift under the slightest weight. Talus hopping is an art, and it certainly helps to wear sticky-rubber approach shoes. Boulders with lichen, especially when wet after a typical afternoon thunderstorm, can become astoundingly slick. A broken or twisted ankle or even a smashed shin can put a quick end to a session.

Frigid Water: The lakes and rivers are just above freezing cold and many don't thaw out until July. Hypothermia from swimming in the cold water is a very serious threat, as is the utter shock to the system when submerged in an alpine lake.

Thunderstorms: In the summer months, when the Park and Mt. Evans are most popular, these areas are plagued by thunderstorms. They often roll in around 1 pm and can linger all evening. Occasionally, the weather will clear, even after the most vicious of storms, and an amazing evening session can be had. It is very important to find cover of some sort if a storm approaches and to keep a sharp eye on the weather. The best places to go are low-lying areas in dense trees, although no spot is free of danger. Sitting underneath a boulder can keep one dry, but it is a dangerous place to be, as lightning can jump from the bottom of the boulder, through you, and to the ground. Sit on your crashpad if possible. Mostly the storms will come from the west, and can be upon the inattentive climber before they realize what has happened. It is

Clouds gathering in Upper Chaos Canyon, RMNP

Lightning strikes the flanks of Mt. Evans during a typical summer storm

no fun being in a thunderstorm in Upper Chaos Canyon with no shelter. Every climber should bring with them a waterproof rain jacket every time they head into the mountains. Hypothermia, the condition in which the core body temperature lowers below 95 degress, is a dangerous threat to those without a rain jacket. A cotton t-shirt or sweatshirt can exacerbate the situation, even on seemingly mild but wet days, as wet cotton absorbs 100% of the heat given off by the body. It can snow any month of the year at the high elevations in the Park.

Snowpack: Climbers visiting in the early season can take advantage of the high level of the snowpack. Snow drifts from a heavy winter can pile 15–20 ft in the boulders. While this buries most of the best problems well into summer, it makes it easier to navigate and can smooth out dangerous landings. It also can hide holes that one can easily fall into, make steep slopes very slippery, and get everything wet. The composition of the snow can vary from day to day in the spring, when it melts quickly.

Hypothermia: Hypothermia is a very serious condition that can occur when a person is cold and wet, and their core body temperature drops. It can be 30 or 40 degrees colder in RMNP than Boulder or Denver and 20 to 30 degrees colder than Estes Park or Idaho Springs. If there is one rule to go by, it is that the mountains are extremely unpredictable and every climber should always be prepared for the worst. Pay attention to the weather at all times. Always bring a rain jacket.

A Note About Water

During the summer, there is a water source at the Bear Lake Parking Area in RMNP, near the bus stop shelter. This is shut off for the winter around September 1. There is no water source at Mt. Evans. Some climbers bring water filters or iodine tablets to purify water when they arrive at the boulders. Giardia lives in many, if not all of the rivers and lakes in RMNP and Mt. Evans. It is acquired by drinking unfiltered water. It is a nasty parasite which can leave one sick for weeks. If you drink unfiltered water from the rivers or lakes in RMNP or Mt. Evans, there is a good chance it will make you sick. It is imperative to stay hydrated at altitude.

Gear—The Eleven Essentials
Every climber should bring with them, every time....

- ❑ Crashpad (the bigger the better)
- ❑ Sticky-soled approach/hiking shoes for rock-hopping
- ❑ Rain jacket
- ❑ Hat
- ❑ Sunscreen
- ❑ Headlamp
- ❑ Adequate clothing for cold & windy weather
- ❑ Food and water for all day
- ❑ Map
- ❑ Lip Balm
- ❑ Guidebook!

Seasonal Information

June

The season for the alpine areas (Upper Chaos, Lower Chaos and Emerald Lake, Area A and Area B) begins in earnest around June 1, although many problems can remain buried well into July. Climbers visiting the Park before June should expect to dig things out, to hike in waist-deep soft snow, and to be prepared for winter conditions. Climbers visiting in June should expect walking on packed snow in RMNP and for there to be snow at Mt. Evans, but for most things to be climbable. Conditions can be cool during this month, although many problems are still buried, depending on snow levels. Area A is mostly free of snow by the middle of June.

July

July is the warmest month in the Park and Mt. Evans. This is when the mosquitos come out in full force, and the snow melts surprisingly fast. Conditions in Lower Chaos can be warm and muggy, but evenings can be good. It can be downright hot at The Dali Boulder of Mt. Evans as temperatures in the Front Range can soar into the 100s. Upper Chaos and the Hallet Boulder are the best choice. Parking is rarely an issue at Mt. Evans, but this is prime tourist season for the Park. The Bear Lake Parking Lot is often full by 9:30 am. The parking can stay this way until fall.

August

August can also be a warm month, but fall is coming soon. This is the time when thunderstorms can get nasty, but towards the end of the month things begin to cool off. The monsoons bring short rain showers every afternoon most of the month, but things start to dry out moving into September. These showers can last all day, or can be quite brief. The rock dries out quickly at Mt. Evans and RMNP and it is possible to be climbing just a few minutes after even the most intense rains.

September

The beginning of prime bouldering season in RMNP. The parking lot can be very busy during the weekends, but empty during the week. The aspen turn golden yellow toward the middle and the end of the month. A great time to be out bouldering. Upper Chaos Canyon conditions are perfect, and the threat from storms is much lower as the cool, dry air moves in. Area B is a great place to be this time of year.

October

For the hardcore boulderer this is the best time to be in RMNP. Snow in the high country begins to threaten. By the end of October, Upper Chaos is totally covered in snow, and most likely, so is Lower. For the lucky climber, there can still be crisp days, although things can be shut down at any moment this late in the year. Emerald Lake could potentially be climbable all year, however brutally cold temperatures, strong winds, and heavy snow make bouldering nearly impossible after Oct. Mt. Evans, being in the trees, is much less susceptible to high winds, and it is usually possible to boulder here until the end of Oct. There are always exceptions to the rule.

Nov-May

Forget about trying to climb in Upper Chaos, Lower Chaos, Emerald Lake or Mt. Evans in the winter. The weather and snow are extremely fickle in the early spring. It is possible to climb at Emerald, occasionally, as early as April or May, but most of Evans and Chaos Canyon remain buried until June.

A great source for checking the weather is:
http://www.nps.gov/romo/photosmultimedia/webcams.htm which provides views of Chaos Canyon, updated every few minutes. Use the Continental Divide view.

	Jan	Feb	Mar	Apr	May	Jun	Jul	Aug	Sep	Oct	Nov	Dec
Estes Park Average Max. Temperature (F)	39	41	46	53	62	73	79	71	77	59	46	40
Estes Park Average Min. Temperature (F)	18	19	23	27	35	42	47	45	39	31	24	18
Idaho Springs Average Max. Temperature (F)	38	41	46	53	62	73	78	76	69	59	45	38
Idaho Springs Average Min. Temperature (F)	8	10	17	23	31	38	43	42	34	24	15	9

Chris Schulte, *Cobra Commander*, Independence Pass, Colorado. © KEITH LADZINSKI

ALPINE GEOLOGY by Hayden Miller

Nearly two billion years of geologic processes led to the present-day boulder fields in the high alpine regions of Colorado. The rocks found in Rocky Mountain National Park and on the flanks of Mt. Evans are a result of the three most broad geologic processes: intrusion, sedimentation and metamorphism. While the two areas share the more recent geologic chapters of uplift and erosion, the geology of the areas also differ in significant ways.

The bouldering in RMNP occurs predominantly on 1.7 billion year old metasedimentary biotite gneiss. However, the history of this rock begins even further in the past. Shale, siltstone, and quartz-rich sandstone were deposited in an ancient, shallow sea between 2.0 and 1.8 billion years ago. Over the course of 130 million years, beginning 1.79 billion years ago, the Colorado Province terrane was accreted into an assemblage that would eventually become the lithosphere of the southwestern United States. This accretion process, which is defined by the addition of material to an existing tectonic plate, provided the conditions necessary to metamorphose these sedimentary deposits. Metamorphism is a fundamental process of geology where heat or pressure causes the mineral composition or texture of a rock to change without that rock entering the liquid phase. The shale and silt metamorphosed into biotite schist while the sandstone became biotite gneiss. Gneiss is a medium to high metamorphic grade defined by the presence of compositional bands of lighter and darker rock. These bands are created by like minerals separating during metamorphism; the lighter bands are composed of more felsic minerals dominated by silica, while iron–and magnesium–rich minerals dominate the darker bands.

Gneiss typically has a coarser grain compared to schists, which have much smaller bands of foliation and a sheen resulting from the major axis of minerals aligning under the pressure, such as mica. The unmetamorphosed boulders of RMNP are primarily granitic rocks from the Longs Peak Batholith, an intrusion of rock which occurred after the regional scale metamorphism.

The bouldering found in the Chicago Lakes Basin of Mt. Evans is a 1.442–billion–year–old granodiorite called the Mt. Evans batholith. The Mount Evans batholith is distinguished from other granitic batholiths of similar age in the region because it is considerably more mafic in composition. Granodiorite is a granatoid rock defined by a greater proportion of plagioclase feldspar, a silicate mineral found in felsic igneous rocks, over potasium feldspar. The main minerals founds in the Mt. Evans batholith are oligoclase (a plagioclase feldspar), microcline (a potassium feldspar), quartz, and biotite. In addition, the Mt. Evans batholith contains titanite and magnetite, which are the more mafic minerals. The Mt. Evans batholith also has many veins running through its host. These veins constitute ~5% of the overall rock volume. These veins are called pegmatites and form from the injection of water-saturated magmas. Pegmatites are extremely coarse and often very felsic, which result in a noticeable different texture from the host rock. The pegmatites found at Mt. Evans are primarily aplite in nature, meaning they are dominated by just quartz and feldspar. The pink bands bisecting the Dali Wall are classic examples of pegmatites.

The banded gneiss for which RMNP has become famous

The south face of Hallett Peak

Following the metamorphism found in RMNP and the granitic intrusion exposed at Mt. Evans, nearly a billion years of geologic history occured that had little effect on creating the environment found today. An ocean again covered the continent during the Paleozoic, followed by the formation of the Ancestral Rocky Mountains ~300 million years ago, a mountain chain comparable in size to that of today's Rockies. However, time passed and these ancestral mountains were slowly eroded away by water, wind, and ice. By the Jurassic, ~150 million years ago, the middle of the North American continent was once again under a shallow sea.

Beginning 70 million years ago, in the late Cretaceous, tectonic forces began uplifting the region. Intense stress from the subduction zone along the western edge of the North American plate had translated 1000 miles east into the center of the continent. The heavier oceanic crust of the now extinct Farallon plate was getting pushed underneath the less dense continental crust at an unusually shallow angle that caused the tectonic forces to trigger uplift near the center of the continent. This tectonic activity has created a plethora of folds and faults along the Colorado Front Range.

While erosion has been an active process since the formation of the Rocky Mountains, the climatic events of the very recent geologic past have had the greatest impact on creating the environment seen today. The existence of permanent bodies of ice is an extremely rare occurrence in the Earth's history but a very powerful erosive agent. Two periods of glaciation have shaped the valleys and peaks of the Rocky Mountains, to expose the steep rock walls that many of the boulders climbed today originate from. The Bull Lake (peak glaciation 123,000 years ago) and Pinedale (peak glaciation 23,500 to 20,500 years ago) formed many of the U-shaped valleys found in Colorado, such as that of the Chicago Lakes Basin. The sharp rise in topography between Lower Chicago Lake and Upper Chicago Lake is a knickpoint caused by a temporary pause in the glacier's retreat as temperatures warmed. These glaciers left large rock faces exposed after their retreat. Because of the young nature of these faces and the intense forces experienced during glaciation, pieces broke off and cascaded down to the valley floor. When the broken rock is larger in size, it is referred to as talus, and can be so prevalent that few places of the original valley floor are still exposed, such as Upper Chaos Canyon. However, it is more common to have smaller clusters of talus in places such as is found in the Chicago Lakes Basin of Mt. Evans.

Further Reading:

Kellogg, Karl S., Bryant Bruce, and Reed, John C. Jr. ***The Colorado Front Range – Anatomy of a Laramide uplift***.

Aleinikoff, John N, Reed Jr., John C, DeWitt, Ed. ***The Mount Evans batholith in the Colorado Front Rage: Revision of its age and reinterpretation of its structure.***

Cole, James C. and William A. Braddock. Geologic Map of the Estes Park 30' x 60' Quadrangle, North Central Colorado.

FAUNA AND FLORA

Fauna and Flora of Mt. Evans and RMNP

The Rocky Mountains are home to all kinds of unique and interesting animals. There are 66 species of mammals in the Park alone. The region was once home to grizzly bear, grey wolf and bison, but they are now locally extinct and the wolverine and lynx are considered extremely rare or potentially extinct as well.

Elk (Cervaus canadensis) number over 3200 in the Park in the summer and are easily spotted. They are an icon of the Estes Park region. They also inhabit the valleys surrounding Mt. Evans, but in far fewer quantities. The fall is mating season for the elk, and their distinct bugles can be heard from the boulders. Keep your distance when observing or photographing these majestic creatures. A large bull elk can weigh 800 pounds.

Black bear (Ursus americanus) are common throughout the Park and in the forests of Mt. Evans. They have been spotted in the boulders of Chaos Canyon, and on the trail to the boulders. If you happen to be lucky enough to see a black bear, do not run. Stop, stay calm, and make lots of noise, by shouting or clapping your hands. Back away slowly. There are no grizzly bears in the Mt. Evans Wilderness Area or RMNP.

Mountain lion (Puma concolor) sightings are rare, although there is a healthy population of the cats at both locations. They are most active from dusk until dawn. If you see a mountain lion, remain calm and do not run. Do all that you can to appear bigger, and if you are attacked, fight back.

Marmot (Marmota flaviventris) can be spotted in the higher elevations, and occasionally in Upper Chaos Canyon. They are common above the treeline at Mt. Evans. They are harmless, but curious creatures. They weigh between 5–11 pounds. They are a genus (Marmota) of the squirrel.

Pika (Ochotona princeps) are often confused with marmots. They are much smaller, 7 or 8 inches in length and are known for their distinctly high-pitched chirp.

Moose (Alces alces) are huge animals, standing 6 feet at the shoulders. They are extremely unpredictable, and can run 35 miles per hour. Females are extremely protective of their young. Back away slowly and never approach these majestic beasts.

Mountain goats (Oreamnos americanus) are not found in RMNP, but are found on the steep slopes around Mt. Evans. They can be spotted late in the year on the cliffs about Area A and B, as they make their way down from the summit as winter approaches.

Other animals that may be spotted are bighorn sheep, pine marten (which is a long and dark weasel-like creature and can be seen in Chaos Canyon on a somewhat regular basis), porcupine, coyote, mule deer, beaver and snowshoe hare.

A mountain goat grazes on tundra near the shore of Wolverineland

The wilderness areas are also home to a variety of interesting plant life. The Colorado columbine is a common sight during the summer months and it is the state flower. Approximately 30% of RMNP is alpine tundra, which is a tract of treeless land at very high elevations. The tundra is home to a number of alpine flowers, including moss, lanceleaf chiming bells, wallflower, forget-me-not, and avens. Repeated footsteps on this fragile ground can easily destroy these plants for hundreds of years. Take care when walking above the treeline.

The dense forests below the treeline are comprised of lodgepole pines, spruce and douglas fir. There are also deciduous aspen, which turn brilliantly golden in late September every year. Their quaking leaves are an icon of the Colorado mountains.

Bristlecone pines live on the shoulders of Mt. Evans. These hardy trees live in cold, dry climates and are some of the oldest living things on earth, and the ones near the Goliath Visitor Center, up the Mt. Evans Scenic Hwy, are 1,700 years old. They are not found in RMNP.

It is inappropriate and against Park and Wilderness rules to approach or feed wildlife. If you are stopping on the trail or road to photograph an animal, please be courteous to other tourists, get out of the way and pull over.

Colorado columbines bloom near the summit of Mt. Evans

Elk come down from the high country in early spring, RMNP

Like Lists? Start ticking.
The Best of the Best

☑ Worth the Hike
☑ Must Dos

The Adventurers List

For the boulderer seeking a unique experience in the wilderness, these problems represent the ultimate in alpine bouldering adventure. They may be highball, or found in remote corners of the mountains, or perhaps are just difficult to access. The climber that ticks this list has demonstrated a high level of commitment to alpine bouldering. Only 3- and 4-star problems were chosen.

Mt. Evans

- ❒ Timeline V1 ★★★
- ❒ The Ladder V1 ★★★★
- ❒ Dripping Wax V3 ★★★
- ❒ Puddle Jumper V3★★★
- ❒ Last Dance V7 ★★★
- ❒ Peasants into Leaders V7 ★★★★
- ❒ Submerged Boulder V8 ★★★
- ❒ Laying in Wait V8 ★★★
- ❒ City Walls of Dying Dreams V10 ★★★
- ❒ Sunseeker V13 ★★★★

RMNP

- ❒ Trout Fishing in America V1 ★★★
- ❒ Green Slab V1 ★★★
- ❒ Emerald Edges V4 ★★★
- ❒ The Hills Have Eyes V4 ★★★
- ❒ Brimstone V6 ★★★
- ❒ The Example V2 ★★★
- ❒ Blade of Glory V7 ★★★
- ❒ Cookies Corner V7 ★★★
- ❒ El Capitan V7 ★★★
- ❒ Golden Ice V7 ★★★★
- ❒ Face Full of Mez V9 ★★★
- ❒ Pterodactyl Stand V9 ★★★
- ❒ Real Large V9 ★★★
- ❒ Full Chaos V10 ★★★★
- ❒ Lonestar (aka Stinkbug) V10 ★★★
- ❒ Weeping Willlow V10 ★★★
- ❒ Whispers of Wisdom V10 ★★★★
- ❒ Eternia V11 ★★★
- ❒ I comb my Hair Like God V11 ★★★
- ❒ Never Never Land V11 ★★★
- ❒ Veritas Sit V11 ★★★★
- ❒ Both Sides of the Spectrum V12 ★★★★

The Best V7 and Under

Mt. Evans and RMNP are well known for their difficult problems. However, there are a number of awesome easier lines as well. This is a list of the best lines which get 3 or 4 stars and are V7 and under.

Mt. Evans

- ❒ V1 (Roadside Boulder #2) ★★★
- ❒ Arête V1 (Roadside Boulder #1) ★★★
- ❒ The Ladder V2 ★★★★
- ❒ Timeline V1 ★★★
- ❒ Warm Up V1 (Warm Up Boulder) ★★★
- ❒ Last of the Ohitians V2 ★★★
- ❒ Puddle Jumper V3 ★★★
- ❒ The Dark Crystal V3 ★★★
- ❒ The B Seam V4 ★★★
- ❒ Drizzle Piss V7 ★★★
- ❒ Last Dance V7 ★★★
- ❒ Peasants into Leaders V7 ★★★★

RMNP

- ❒ Green Slab V1 ★★★
- ❒ Molloy V1 ★★★
- ❒ Trout Fishing in America V1 ★★★
- ❒ The Example V2 ★★★
- ❒ Warm Up Right V3 ★★★
- ❒ Beginner's Luck V3 ★★★
- ❒ Autobot V5 ★★★
- ❒ Skyscraper V5 ★★★★
- ❒ The Kind V5 ★★★★
- ❒ Vacationland V5 ★★★
- ❒ Brimstone V6 ★★★
- ❒ Hanging Arête V6 ★★★
- ❒ The Cube Boulder V6 ★★★
- ❒ Tommy's Arête V7 ★★★
- ❒ V7 ★★★ (Right of Brimstone)
- ❒ Blade of Glory V7 ★★★
- ❒ Cookies Corner V7 ★★★
- ❒ El Capitan (From low) V7 ★★★
- ❒ Golden Ice V7 ★★★★

RMNP and Mt. Evans Best

This is a list of all the 3–and 4–star problems in the guide. It represents the best of the best. This is a list to aspire to, dream about, and hopefully, one day, complete. Only a true master can lay claim to having done all 87 problems.

Mt. Evans

- ❐ V1 (Roadside Boulder #1) ★★★
- ❐ V1 (Roadside Boulder #2) ★★★
- ❐ The Ladder V2 ★★★★
- ❐ Timeline V1 ★★★
- ❐ Warm Up V1 (Warm Up Boulder) ★★★
- ❐ Last of the Ohitians V2 ★★★
- ❐ Dripping Wax V3 ★★★
- ❐ Puddle Jumper V3 ★★★
- ❐ The Dark Crystal V3 ★★★
- ❐ The B Seam V4 ★★★
- ❐ Dripping Wax V3 ★★★
- ❐ Drizzle Piss V7 ★★★
- ❐ Peasants into Leaders V7 ★★★★
- ❐ V8 (Submerged Boulder) ★★★
- ❐ Laying in Wait V8 ★★★
- ❐ Overloard V8 ★★★
- ❐ Seurat V8 ★★★
- ❐ The Dali V8 ★★★
- ❐ Robbery Train V9 ★★★
- ❐ Ginsu V9 ★★★
- ❐ Bierstadt V10 ★★★
- ❐ City Walls of Dying Dreams V10 ★★★
- ❐ Conspicuous Consumption V10 ★★★
- ❐ Gorillas in the Mist V10 ★★★
- ❐ Hume Problem V9 ★★★
- ❐ Public Execution V10 ★★★
- ❐ Silverback V10 ★★★
- ❐ Tactical Error V10 ★★★★
- ❐ Chrome V12 ★★★
- ❐ No More Greener Grasses V12 ★★★★
- ❐ The 1%er V13 ★★★
- ❐ Sunseeker V13 ★★★★
- ❐ Ode to the Modern Man V14 ★★★

RMNP

- ❐ Green Slab V1 ★★★
- ❐ Molloy V1 ★★★
- ❐ Trout Fishing in America V1 ★★★
- ❐ The Example V2 ★★★
- ❐ Beginner's Luck V3 ★★★
- ❐ Warm Up Right V3 ★★★
- ❐ The Hills Have Eyes V4 ★★★
- ❐ Autobot V5 ★★★
- ❐ Skyscraper V5 ★★★★
- ❐ The Kind V5 ★★★★
- ❐ Vacationland V5 ★★★
- ❐ Brimstone V6 ★★★
- ❐ Hanging Arête V6 ★★★
- ❐ The Cube Boulder V6 ★★★
- ❐ Tommy's Arête V7 ★★★
- ❐ V7 ★★★ (Right of Brimstone)
- ❐ Blade of Glory V7 ★★★
- ❐ Cookies Corner V7 ★★★
- ❐ El Capitan (From low) V7 ★★★
- ❐ Golden Ice V7 ★★★★
- ❐ Skipper D V8 ★★★
- ❐ Contents Under Pressure V9 ★★★
- ❐ Dave's Problem V9 ★★★
- ❐ Easy on the Eyes V9 ★★★
- ❐ Face Full of Mez V9 ★★★
- ❐ Large V9 ★★★
- ❐ Memoirs of the Invisible Climber V9 ★★★
- ❐ Pterodactyl Stand V9 ★★★
- ❐ Real Large V9 ★★★
- ❐ Full Chaos V10 ★★★★
- ❐ Lonestar (aka Stinkbug) V10 ★★★
- ❐ Riddles in the Dark V10 ★★★
- ❐ Storm Shadow Stand V10 ★★★
- ❐ Triple Threat V10 ★★★
- ❐ Whispers of Wisdom V10 ★★★★
- ❐ Bring the Ruckus V11 ★★★
- ❐ Dead Raccoon V11 ★★★
- ❐ Eternia V11 ★★★
- ❐ Gobot V11 ★★★
- ❐ I Comb my Hair Like God V11 ★★★
- ❐ L. El Jorge V11 ★★★
- ❐ Never Never Land V11 ★★★
- ❐ Returnia V11 ★★★
- ❐ Veritas Sit V11 ★★★★
- ❐ Both Sides of the Spectrum V12 ★★★★
- ❐ Pterodactyl V12 ★★★
- ❐ Riddles in the Park V12 ★★★
- ❐ Stranger in a Strange Land V12 ★★★
- ❐ Veritas Low Left V12 ★★★
- ❐ Don't Get Too Greedy V13 ★★★
- ❐ Nuthin but Sunshine V13 ★★★
- ❐ Top Notch V13 ★★★
- ❐ Jade V14 ★★★
- ❐ Hypnotized Minds V15 ★★★

Part 1 Mt. Evans

Matt Wilder sends Ode to the Modern Man V14 Photo by Ryan Olson

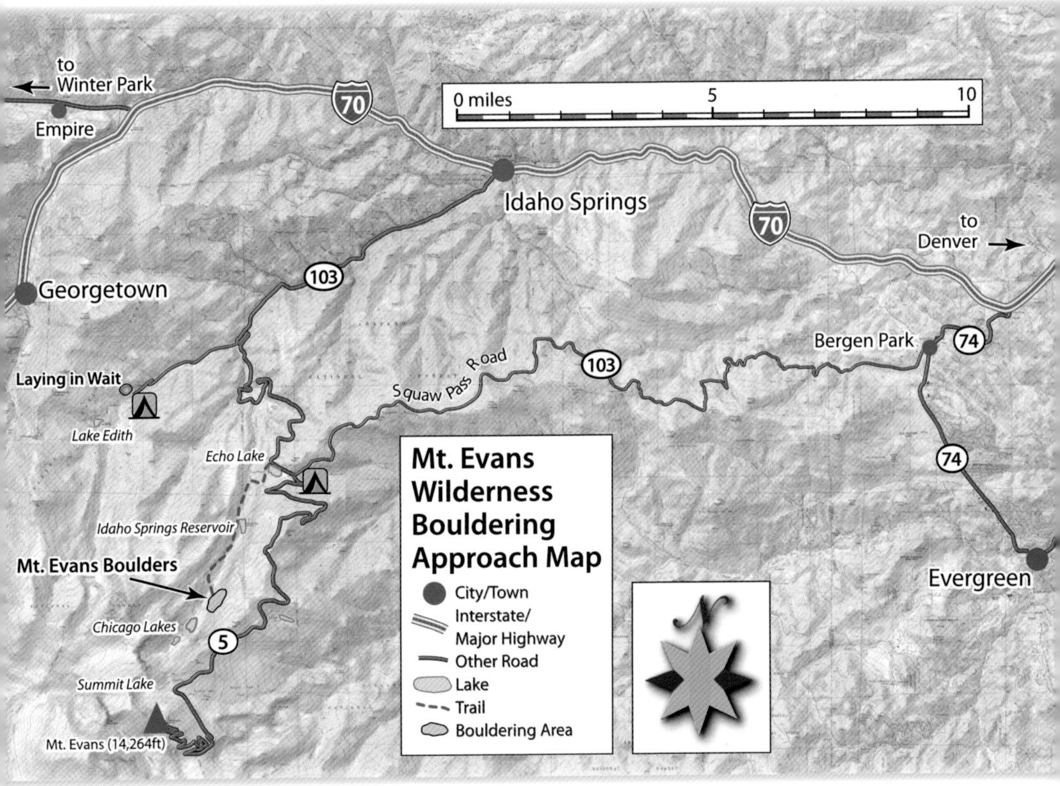

Mt. Evans: The Stats

The bouldering at Mt. Evans lies within the Mt. Evans Wilderness Area. It encompasses 74,401 acres in the Rocky Mountains. The highest point is the summit of Mt. Evans itself, which is 14,264 ft. It is one of the few places in the Lower 48 where tundra is found, and it is home to some of the best alpine bouldering in the country.

Getting There

Climbers visiting internationally should use Denver International Airport (DIA). From DIA follow Pena Blvd for 3.5 miles to I-70 and Denver. From Denver continue west on I-70 39 miles to Idaho Springs. Take Mt. Evans exit 240 and turn left, onto CO 103. If approaching from the west, take I-70 E to the Mt. Evans Exit 240 and turn right onto CO 103. Just south of I-70 is the Clear Creek Ranger Station, on the right. Idaho Springs is on the north side of the freeway and is the last place to get groceries or gasoline before driving to the bouldering area.

To continue on to the bouldering areas take CO 103 south (away from Idaho Springs) for 14 miles to Echo Lake Park, on the right. There are two places to park here, the first being the gravel parking lot on the right, adjacent to Echo Lake (see map on page 30). The second area, which makes for a slightly shorter approach, is accessed by turning right down a dirt road at the close end of the parking lot and following this for a quarter mile to another smaller parking area. Either one is good for parking, although the smaller lot at the end of the dirt road can fill up on a busy summer weekend. It is also possibe to approach from the east on CO 103 out of Bergen Park, although this route is winding and slow.

It is free to park at Echo Lake, and there is no fee required to hike to the boulders.

Mt. Evans Accomodations

Idaho Springs is the closest town to the bouldering. It is a small mining community turned ski-town gateway with a population of 1,889. It sits at an elevation of 7,526 ft. There isn't much in Idaho Springs, but it does serve as the last stopping point for many who visit the Mt. Evans Wilderness Area. It is home to the district ranger station as well. There are gas stations at either end of the town, a Safeway, Subway, McDonalds and numerous other places to eat along Miner St, which is the main street through town.

Idaho Springs has several hotels, and you can always find everything you need just 30 minutes down I-70 E in Denver. Expect to pay $100 a night for a hotel room. For many climbers on a budget, this is simply not an option. There are, however, several places in the area to camp.

Camping

There are several pay sites near the bouldering of Mt. Evans.

Echo Lake Campground:	18 sites	Elevation 10,600 ft	$10 a day
West Chicago Creek Campground:	18 sites	Elevation 9,600 ft	$10 a day
Guanella Pass:	18 sites	Elevation 10,900ft,	$11 a day

Guanella Pass, which is 10 miles south of Georgetown,CO, is also home to a small collection of very nice boulders which are worth a visit if time permits.

Camping is permitted in the boulders at Area A and B, provided a free permit is filled out at the kiosk near the entrance of the Mt. Evans Wilderness Area, just beyond the Idaho Springs Reservoir. Campers must be 100 ft from rivers, lakes, trails, or streams. Fires are allowed here as well, and they too must be 100 ft from rivers, lakes trails or streams. It is best to use an existing fire ring. Dogs are welcome in the Wilderness Area so long as they are on a leash at all times. Waking up in the boulders and having a quiet morning session can be a rewarding experience. Please be respectful and appreciative of this special opportunity.

In the summer, food and drinks can be purchased at the Echo Lake Lodge, which is 0.25 miles beyond the Echo Lake Park (14 miles from Idaho Springs). There is no gas station at the Echo Lake Lodge.

Food

The days at Mt. Evans tend to be long. There are a number of recommended places to fuel up before or after your climbing day.

Buffalo Restaurant: This is the best place to go for dinner after a long day in the wilderness. Buffalo burgers are their specialty. Relatively cheap pub fare. 1817 Miner St., Idaho Springs, CO, 303-567-2729

Two Brothers Deli: Great place for coffee in the morning. They also serve breakfast sandwiches and have free wireless internet. 1424 Miner St., Idaho Springs, CO www.twobrothersdeli.com

Tommyknocker Brewery: A popular place for climbers to eat, although perhaps not the best food in town. Good beer. 1401 Miner St., Idaho Springs, CO, 303-567-2688 www.tommyknocker.com/idahoSprings.htm

Safeway: A large grocery store with all manner of popular food items. 2425 Milner St., Idaho Springs, CO 303-567-2496

Beau Jo's: A place to eat mass quantities of pizza. 1517 Milner St., Idaho Springs, CO 303-567-4376

Things to do / Rest Days

Mt. Evans Summit Road Drive: For those with extra time on their hands, it would be remiss not to take a drive up the Mt. Evans Scenic Highway. Drive 0.25 miles beyond Echo Lake Park, passing Echo Lake on the right. The Echo Lake Lodge is on the right, past the lake. There is no gas here, but snacks can be purchased and in the summer a restaurant is open for business. It is $10 to drive up the road for the day and $25 for the year. The scenery is spectacular as the road winds its way precariously up into the tundra to a parking area just 200 ft from the summit. Keep an eye out for hikers, road bikers, bighorn sheep, and mountain goats. Driving up the road during a storm can be thrilling, but beware of the dangers of lightning, as there is little cover above the treeline.

Hiking: There are plenty of great trails to hike in the Mt. Evans Wilderness Area. Continuing on past Area A and B on the Chicago Lakes Trail No. 52 leads to the Lower and Upper Chicago Lakes. More climbing opportunities abound, and as the trail heads above the treeline, the scenery is incredible. Hiking up to this basin is well worth the effort. There are also many opportunities to hike off of the Mt. Evans Scenic Highway, including Lincoln Lake, Summit Lake and the short hike to the actual summit of the mountain.

Bouldering in the Mt. Evans Wilderness

By Ralph Brandt, Mt. Evans Wilderness Ranger

At first glance, bouldering might seem to be an ideal form of Wilderness climbing. No hardware, no fixed anchors, no ropes — just shoes, a little chalk, and perhaps a crashpad to ease that sudden return to earth. Indeed, a couple folks wandering from boulder to boulder checking out problems generally have little impact. However, the reality is that the repeated use of a popular bouldering area by a large number of boulderers can quickly have a significant impact on the environment. Repeated footsteps wear down the vegetation between the boulders and the underlying soil begins to erode away. Dozens of chalked hands turn the stone white, and loose chalk spills out from chalkbags onto the ground. Seemingly insignificant individual impacts are cumulative and often become major problems in a surprisingly short time. Congressionally designated Wilderness areas, like Mount Evans, are set aside to be preserved in their natural condition with minimal evidence of human disturbance. Along Colorado's Front Range corridor, close proximity to large population centers makes preservation of wild natural areas, designated Wilderness or not, particularly challenging. So what can individual boulderers, and the bouldering community as a whole, do to minimize their impact and preserve these areas? Most of what can be done falls under the principles of Leave No Trace:

Plan Ahead

Know what the regulations and specific concerns for the area are. On public lands, most regulations are in place to protect the environment. Specific concerns, such as fragile alpine tundra, or habitat of threatened or endangered species, vary from place to place.

Utilize Durable Surfaces

While travelling to and from an area, or from problem to problem, stay on established routes that have already been impacted. If the area shows little impact, step from rock to rock, spread out your group, and avoid walking across and crushing live vegetation. This is important anywhere, but particularly on fragile alpine tundra. Avoid short, steep routes in favor of longer, more gentle slopes. If the route is muddy, walk through the mud rather than around the edge to keep from making a bigger mud hole. If you're a member of a small group, sit on a rock or log, not on the vegetation, while resting, watching, or waiting your turn on a problem.

Dispose of Waste Properly

Leave the area as you found it (or better). Pack out all litter, yours and others, that you find in the area and on your way in or out. Minimize use of chalk, avoid spills, and if spills happen, clean them up. Solid human waste should, at a minimum, be buried in cat holes six to eight inches deep, and the toilet paper packed out. The truly enlightened, virtuous boulderer will pack out everything.

Leave What You Find as You Find It

Modifying the environment to suit your needs or desires is selfish and unacceptable. Bouldering should be little more than you and nature. You can modify yourself through training and practice, and improve your ability to stick with sticky rubber and the sparing use of chalk, but modifying or "improving" nature damages the resource and runs contrary to the ideal of the climber working through the problem as presented. Examples include removing trees or pruning branches to open up a problem or improve a landing, or creating or "improving" a hold on a problem. If you find a problem behind a tree, the tree is part of the problem, not something to be pruned or removed. The challenge of a hold with a plant growing behind it is to use the hold without disturbing the plant. Let problems remain as you find them.

Respect Wildlife

Most Wilderness areas, Mount Evans included, require that dogs be on a leash, primarily for the protection of wildlife, but also for other users, not all of whom like to be approached by a strange dog running loose. If you don't feel that you can comply with this, please leave your dog at home.

Be Considerate of Other Visitors

People head out into the woods for many reasons, often to escape the chaos of the city and find peace in nature. This is particularly the case in Wilderness, where it's expected that one can find a natural setting and an opportunity for solitude. Avoid loud voices and noise, and leave your music behind.

A Few Additional Concerns for Boulderers

One problem, which has occurred in the past in bouldering areas in the Mount Evans Wilderness, is the stashing of equipment, crash pads in particular, overnight or longer. While it may be an inconvenience to carry them in and out with you on every visit, that's part of the game. Gear stashed behind boulders and under rocks is found by mice, marmots, and other critters, who quickly set to chewing on your expensive gear. This isn't particularly good for you, who will have to replace your expensive gear, and is very harmful to the wildlife, whose native diet doesn't include nylon, vinyl, or foam rubber. Further, bits of your chewed up gear end up spread around the area as litter. In the 1964 Wilderness Act, Wilderness is defined as (among other things), a place "where man himself is a visitor who does not remain." That goes for your stuff, too.

One of the most troubling recent aspects of some of the bouldering in the Mount Evans Wilderness has been rapidly increasing use due to the amount of publicity that has been given to some of these areas. While sharing adventures and information with friends is only natural, please consider the effect that increased publicity, such as in the climbing press or on the internet, is likely to have on the amount of use and impact these areas get. We avoid publicizing areas we're trying to preserve, which is why commercial filming of any kind in Wilderness is rarely permitted. When excessive impacts occur due to overuse, management actions and restrictions must be considered to protect the Wilderness resource.

Public lands belong to us all and we all have the right to enjoy those lands, as long as in doing so we don't damage them for those who follow us. The human pressures on our public lands, particularly in these areas so close to the population centers of the Front Range, are tremendous. We all have to practice thoughtful stewardship of our wild landscapes or what we value in them won't be able to last for long.

Seth Allred barely edges out Boulder local Christian Griffith for the FA of Chrome V12. Griffith repeated the line soon after. Not pictured is Adam Henry, who couldn't make it up the long hike. Photo by Caroline Treadway

A mountain goat perches precariously on the broken cliffs above Area A

Mt. Evans Wilderness Area Bouldering Etiquette

Bouldering in the Mt. Evans Wilderness Area is a privilege and we should do everything we can to preserve and protect the resource and our opportunity to climb there. If we can help the rangers then they can help us. It is the responsibility of every visitor to know the rules and regulations that govern the Mt. Evans Wilderness Area. The rangers here have worked with climbers in the past, and are happy to see people enjoying the wilderness in this way. Remember, you are in an area regulated by the federal government, and breaking the law is a federal offense. There are several key differences between a National Park and a Wilderness Area, although it is imperative that both areas are treated with respect.

Stashing gear, including crashpads, overnight is forbidden by Wilderness Area rules. This is one issue the rangers have been very outspoken about, and it is the number one thing climbers can do to maintain the good relationship that exists between the rangers and climbers. DON'T STASH YOUR PAD.

Climbers should not drive up the road, and while there is a legal way to aquire a key for one day, the rangers have asked that EVERY CLIMBER does the hike EVERY TIME. It is the responsibility of each climber to be responsible to the community and to always do the hike.

Pof should never be used. It can permanently change the texture of the rock, especially when mixed with chalk. Chalk (magnesium carbonate) is acceptable.

CHIPPING is absolutely not permitted, as it not only is destructive and weak, it is in violation of Park rules. DO NOT CHIP HOLDS.

CLEAN UP YOUR TRASH. It takes a few seconds to double check an area before you leave, and if you drop a toothbrush or water bottle in among the rocks make a good effort and fish it out.

Cutting down trees or removal of vegetation is strictly forbidden by Wilderness Area rules and regulations.

Do not harass, approach, or feed the wildlife.

You are allowed to camp near the boulders at Area A and B. A free permit is required.

Stay on marked trails or social trails described in the text when possible. Avoid trampling vegetation.

Leave your music at home. While climbers can and do bring iPods with speakers to the boulders, this is often looked down upon, as it intrudes on others ability to enjoy the silence. Remember, many other visitors don't care about your techno music. Headphones make a great compromise. Be respectful of others' right to enjoy the area. The rangers have asked that climbers keep noise pollution at a minimum.

Mt. Evans certainly gets fewer tourists than RMNP, and you will find more local visitors here, nevertheless, they will most certainly ask about the crashpad on your back. Being courteous and taking the time to answer a few quick questions can go a long way toward establishing a positive image. Don't be rude.

The following activities are prohibited in the Mt. Evans Wilderness Area:

Possessing or using a motor vehicle or motorized equipment.

Possessing or using a hang glider or bicycle.

Landing of aircraft, or dropping or picking up of any supplies, materials or persons by aircraft is prohibited.

Having groups of more than 15 persons and/or 10 saddle, pack, or draft animals.

Possessing dogs, unless under physical restraint of a leash.

Camping within 100 feet of trails, lakes, or streams.

Building or using a campfire within 100 feet of trails, rivers, lakes, or streams.

Hitching, hobbling, or tethering saddle, pack, or draft animals within 100 feet of trails, rivers, lakes, or streams.

Possessing, storing, or transporting unprocessed feed for horses or other stock.

Possessing or using a cart, wagon, or other vehicle is prohibited. Wheelchairs suitable for indoor use are exempted.

Shortcutting switchbacks on trails is strictly prohibited.

The flanks of Mt. Evans bathed in evening light

Mt. Evans History

Little is known about the early history of bouldering at Mt. Evans. Evans has often been strangely overlooked as a climbing destination in favor of the numerous and relatively easily accessed objectives in RMNP. After Dave Graham and others began developing RMNP in the summer of 2000, a group of local climbers began to turn their attention to other regions of the Front Range. In 2002, looking for route potential on the stark Black Wall, near the summit of Mt. Evans, Ken Kenny and Rob Pizem spotted some large boulders at the base. They convinced Ben Scott and a number of others to hike down the trail. Ben was floored walking by Areas A and B and quickly returned. The following years Ben spearheaded the development of these stellar bouldering areas. That year Ben put up The Dali V8, Seurat V8, Beirstadt V10, The Ladder V1, Timeline V1 and several other classics. There were only a small number of climbers who even knew about the boulders at this time. Climbers like Dave Ludders, Jason Tarry, Greg Loomis, Chuck Fryberger, Jamie Emerson, Cameron Cross, Clayton Reagan, and Jeremy Bisher were all part of the early crew to develop Mt. Evans. Ben was happy to keep the place a secret, but he knew that eventually the word would get out. In 2003 James Litz made a visit for a day and put up Public Execution V10 and Mental Pollution V10. James originally suggested the later to be V12. Cameron Cross was there and said, "No way!" to which Litz responded, "I did European Human Being second try and this felt harder." He also tried what was then referred to as the Lime Wall Project on the far right side of The Dali Wall. He managed to do the bottom sequence, taking the now famous gaston as a sidepull, moving into a miserable undercling and up to the edges. After ripping through nearly every hard problem in Rocky Mountain National Park, he thought this was potentially a V15. But his effort was only one day, and his fingers were shredded. That year Ben also added the classic slab Laying in Wait V8, just west of Idaho Springs.

In 2004, the word started to trickle out, and Luke Parady made the very significant FA of No More Greener Grasses, the project tried by James Litz the year before. Harry Robertson made the second ascent in an hour, and six days later did the FA of Clear Blue Skies. Originally Clear Blue Skies was harder, perhaps V13, but a key hold crumbled and became larger, and now the consensus seems to have settled around V11. Later that year Randy Puro took advantage of some very cold temperatures and climbed the classic and tricky Silverback V10, just down the hill, and many of the classics were slowly being filled in.

Chip Phillips on Snow White V7, Area A, Mt. Evans

In 2006, Daniel Woods, fresh off of a very quick send of Terre de Siene, the classic V13 in Hueco Tanks, made the first of ascent of the hardest problem on the Dali Boulder, Ode to the Modern Man V14. This remains the hardest problem at Area A or B. Development has continued at Area A at this sporadic pace. Ben Scott returned in 2007 to leave a stunning mark on Area A with his ascent of Peasants into Leaders V7. This is one of the best highballs in America.

Cameron Cross was one of the first climbers to really put effort into things at Area B. He climbed Gorillas in the Mist V10, Robbery Train V9 (a difficult and rarely ascended overhanging roof crack) and, most impressively, City Walls of Dying Dreams V10. City Walls is an obvious and stunning arête, and Cameron's first ascent was one of the best at Area B. Dave Hume also made a one-day visit, climbing the first ascent of the Hume Problem V9. Dave started sitting on the ground, on one pad, and topped out the first ascent in a driving rainstorm, climbing his namesake problem.

Chris Schulte, a reclusive climber, was active at Area A and B in the years from 2005 to 2010. He climbed several overlooked lines, including Ground Control V11 and Child Stars V12 at Area A, and a number of things at Area B, including Gatecrasher V12, Sam Hall V9, and the hardest problem there, the 1%er V13, in the summer of 2010. The greatest contribution was made to Area B in 2009, by Nalle Hukkataival, a visiting Finnish climber. Not only did Nalle climb every problem on the Dali Wall in two days, flashing No More Greener Grasses V12, he hiked up to Area B and made the first ascent of possibly the best problem in Colorado, Sunseeker V13. This incredible problem was found by Greg Loomis in the summer of 2002. The height of the problem, the poor landing and the committing nature of the moves, in addition to the absolutely stunning rock and line made this a long sought-after project. Cameron Cross had done a V10 stand start the previous year, and had even considered rigging a net to fall on. Nalle had the advantage of some deep and well-packed snow.

That same year Dave climbed Big Worm V14, at Area A. This is a classic compression line and one of the hardest in the area. For the women, Alex Puccio made the FFA of Clear Blue Skies V11 in 2008 and Angela Payne climbed the FFA of Silverback V10 and then most impressively, in 2010, No More Greener Grasses V12.

By 2011 most of the main lines at Mt. Evans have been climbed, although there are a few projects hiding in the talus.

Ben Scott runs a lap on his FA Canvas V4, Area A, Mt. Evans

Mt. Evans Bouldering

Approach

Echo Lake is the trailhead for Chicago Lakes Trail No. 52, which leads to the bouldering at Mt. Evans. From the parking lot at Echo Lake, hike around the right (west) shore of Echo Lake on a large, flat trail. At the far end of the lake, head slightly right and uphill, on the Chicago Lakes Trail No. 52. This is an established trail of the Mt. Evans Wilderness Area. Follow the trall west, which is at first relatively flat, then drops steeply down eight switchbacks to Chicago Creek At the bottom of the valley, the trail will bend to the right, cross a small footbridge and then intersect a dirt road, 1.3 miles from the parking lot. Head left on the dirt road for 0.25 miles to the first boulder. Area A (which holds many of the popular problems) is about 3.0 miles from the trailhead and it takes roughly an hour to hike there.

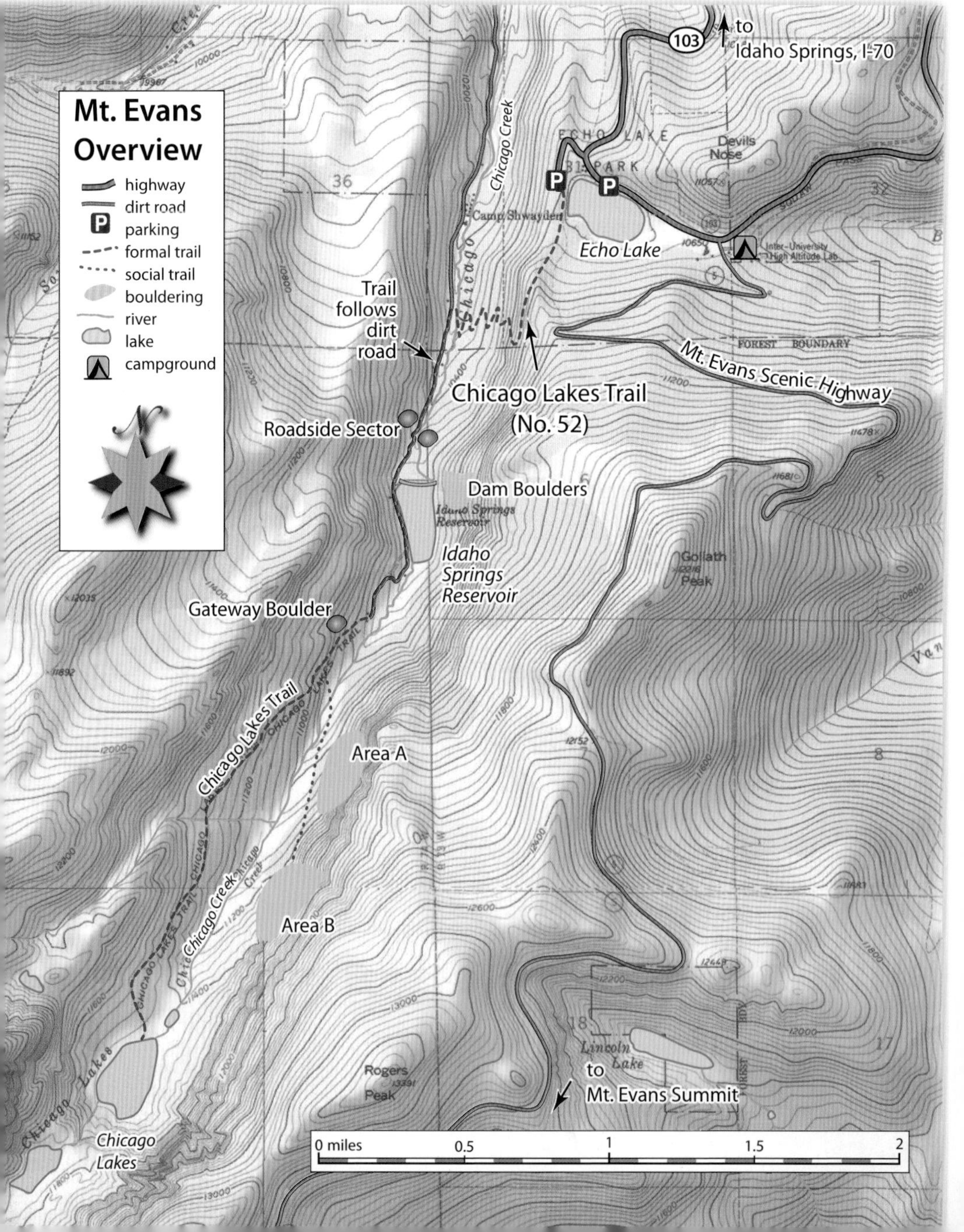

a. payne, rmnp, r. olson photo
ORGANIC
www.organicclimbing.com

Roadside Sector

From the intersection with the dirt road, turn left and hike 0.25 miles up a long hill. Look for a wooden, "Horsetrail" sign with green letters, nailed to a tree on the right. Hike 15 yds into the woods on the faint "Horsetrail," stop, look up and left. Hike up to the large obvious boulder 10 yds away and 1.8 miles from Echo Lake.

A. Roadside Boulder

❒ 1. **V1** ★★★
Stand start. Climb the arête. A great warm-up. Downclimb the adjacent aspen tree to get off the top.
FA Ben Scott

❒ 2. **V1** ★★★
Start standing and traverse from right to left up good holds.

❒ 3. **Tactical Error V10** ★★★★
Sit start on the obvious sloping rail. Climb straight up the compression feature. Excellent.
FA TJ Burchfield 2008

❒ 4. **V3** ★★
Around to the left from Tactical Error. Start on a good edge and head left through some crystals.

❒ 5. **Silver and Glass V11** ★★
Sit start with a flat left-hand edge and a right hand on a very small crystal. Move up to a terrible right-hand sidepull and some nice left-hand slopers.
FA Jamie Emerson 2006

❒ 6. **V3** ★★
Around the left from Silver Glass. Stand start on good underclings and head right.

❒ 7. **Project**
Stand start on underclings, climb up.

B. Warm Up Boulder

Continue past the "Horsetrail" cutoff for the Roadside Boulder and walk 50 yds up the dirt road to a boulder which sits just off the road on the left, 1.9 miles from Echo Lake.

❒ 1. **Arête V9** ★★
Stand start over a poor landing and climb the sloping arête.
FA Ben Scott 2004

❒ 2. **Warm Up V1** ★★★
Stand start on good holds and climb up the incuts. A nice place to take a break.

Warm Up Boulder

Roadside Boulder-Tactical Error

Roadside Boulder-Silver and Glass

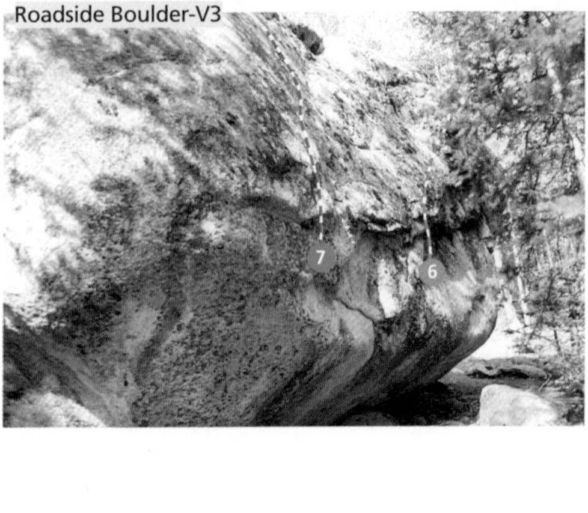

Roadside Boulder-V3

Dam Boulders

The Dam Boulders are a separate cluster set off the road. For those wishing to contine to Area A, skip past this portion of the text and continue on to the Gateway Boulder. Just beyond the Warm Up Boulder the road opens up. About 100 yds beyond the Warm Up Boulder, turn left, off the road and cross a culvert, walking in between two chain link fences. Idaho Springs Reservoir will come into view on your right. Walk 75 yds along the flat top of the dam towards a small cluster of boulders submerged in the reservoir. At the end of the dam, head right, and walk along the shore 20 yds to the first few boulders. It is almost exactly 2 miles from Echo Lake to the Idaho Springs Reservoir.

A. Dam Arête

❒ 1. **Dam Arête V3** ★★
Start on a low jug, with good feet, reach out right to a sloper, and climb up the arête.

Damn Arête

B. Submerged Boulder

❒ 1. **V8** ★★★
Start on a good rail and make a big move up and right to a sloper. This problem was originally done during a very dry year, when the water was low. Weeks after the first ascent it became submerged and has been so ever since.
FA Ben Scott 2002

C. Dripping Wax

❒ 1. **Dripping Wax V3** ★★★
This problem is up in the forest from Dam Arête. It faces the reservoir. Follow a faint social trail straight uphill for 25 yds. Start standing on a right-facing sidepull and climb the amazing highball. An easier version (V1) traverses in from the right. The crux is at the top–For its grade, one of the best problems in the state.
FA Ben Scott 2002

Submerged Boulder

Dripping Wax

The Gateway Boulder

From the dam at the north end of the Idaho Springs Reservoir, continue along the dirt road. Walk past the reservoir on the left, and then two cabins on the left. The road terminates at the Mt. Evans Wilderness Area. Take a moment to fill out a tag as required and read the signs. Continue uphill on the Chicago Lakes Trail No. 52. After a short hill, the trail will flatten out and head slightly downhill, into a meadow. The Gateway Boulder is the obvious erratic on the right side of the path, 2.5 miles from Echo Lake.

The Gateway Boulder

A. The Gateway Boulder

❒ 1. **Black Tornado V7** ★★
Stand start and reach high for a seam.
FA Chip Philips

❒ 2. **Downtrail Face V6** ★★
Sit start on crimps on top of a shield of rock.

❒ 3. **The Horn Arête V6** ★★
Climb the sloping dihedral feature from a stand start. Very sloping and committing at the top.
FA Ben Scott

❒ 4. **Gateway Arête V3** ★★
Start sittng at the base of the arête and climb straight up. The stand start is V0 and makes a great warm-up.

❒ 5. **Gateway Face V4** ★★
Stand start over a poor landing and climb the sloping arête.
FA Jason Tarry

❒ 6. **Gateway V6** ★★
Start standing on sidepulls and climb the arête.
FA Jason Tarry

The Gateway Boulder

Bouldering at Mt. Evans

By Bennett Scott

Enormous granite boulders *everywhere*. My heart starts racing. Upcanyon, downcanyon, large granite boulders fill my view. Is this possible? I swear I'm only a short drive from downtown Denver, and nobody's really climbed on these boulders before.

I first moved to Colorado in the summer of 1998 from the flat lands of Akron, Ohio. Colorado was where the real rock climbers lived and I wanted to see what it was all about. At first I just assumed every single rock had been climbed on by some bad-ass at some point over the years. Pat Goodman, Hank Jones and Will Lemaire opened my eyes to the incredible possibility that there *are* lots of unclimbed boulders in Colorado. With their motivation I began scouring every hillside outside Fort Collins for new boulder problems, and there were plenty.

In 2001 after giving up on a botany degree from CSU (Colorado State University), I enrolled in the Art Institute of Colorado to pursue my idea of doing commercial art for a living. With the Poudre Canyon and Red Feather Lakes being so far away now, I needed a new outlet for my lichen-scrubbing obsession. I started climbing in Boulder more and meeting some of the social misfits that had made bouldering their life's passion. Mike Brooks introduced me to a few guys like Kevin Murphy and Mike Freischlag who took me to some newer spots they had been developing.

Ben Scott with his wife, Sue Scott

One day Kevin told me a story by way of Pete Takeda. Pete had been trad climbing for years on Mt. Evans' famous Black Wall. During that time he had noticed tons of granite boulders that nobody, apparently, had climbed on before. That was all we needed to hear. The next weekend we rallied the troops and drove to Summit Lake. I was a bit skeptical because I just assumed it had all been seen before and Pete was just out of the bouldering loop. After leaving the Summit Lake parking lot we soon reached the rim of the Chicago Lakes Valley and my eyes immediately found the massive talus field well down from Lower Chicago Lake. Oh my God, are those real? The other guys in the group were like, "Yeah, they're good boulders, but who the hell's going to hike all the way back there to go bouldering?" I zipped my lip and complacently shook my head in agreement.

On the way down the trail I was last in line; everyone else was chatting it up and talking about the day's excursion. We walked right past the large fields of talus that would become Areas A and B. No one else in the group seemed to notice. I was spazzing out the whole way, just dumbfounded by the hundreds and hundreds of boulders that couldn't escape my view. In that instant I knew I was going to be very busy developing boulders at Mt. Evans in the coming years.

The next five years were a total blur. Jeremy Bisher, Jason Tarry, David Ludders, Greg Loomis, Cameron Cross, Clayton Reagan, Jamie Emerson, and I began developing one of the best alpine bouldering areas in the country. It was incredible. So many classic lines to pick, so much lichen to scrub, and so many talus landings to fix. It was a ton of work but none of us cared, we felt like kids in a candy store, and couldn't bribe anyone to come get a taste. "No, I'm going to the Park (Rocky Mountain National Park) to work this problem Dave Graham put up" they'd say. We would just smile and wish them good luck on their project. We knew Mt. Evans was awesome and didn't care if anyone else did. Developing Mt. Evans with my friends remains among my best rock climbing memories to this day.

It is a special place that we need to respect as a climbing community. Our impact on this ecosystem is easily noticed and takes hundreds of years to repair. Mt. Evans is a climbing area we need to protect so future generations can have the same amazing experience we get to have today. Please pick up your trash and help educate younger climbers who may not understand how fragile this bouldering area truly is.

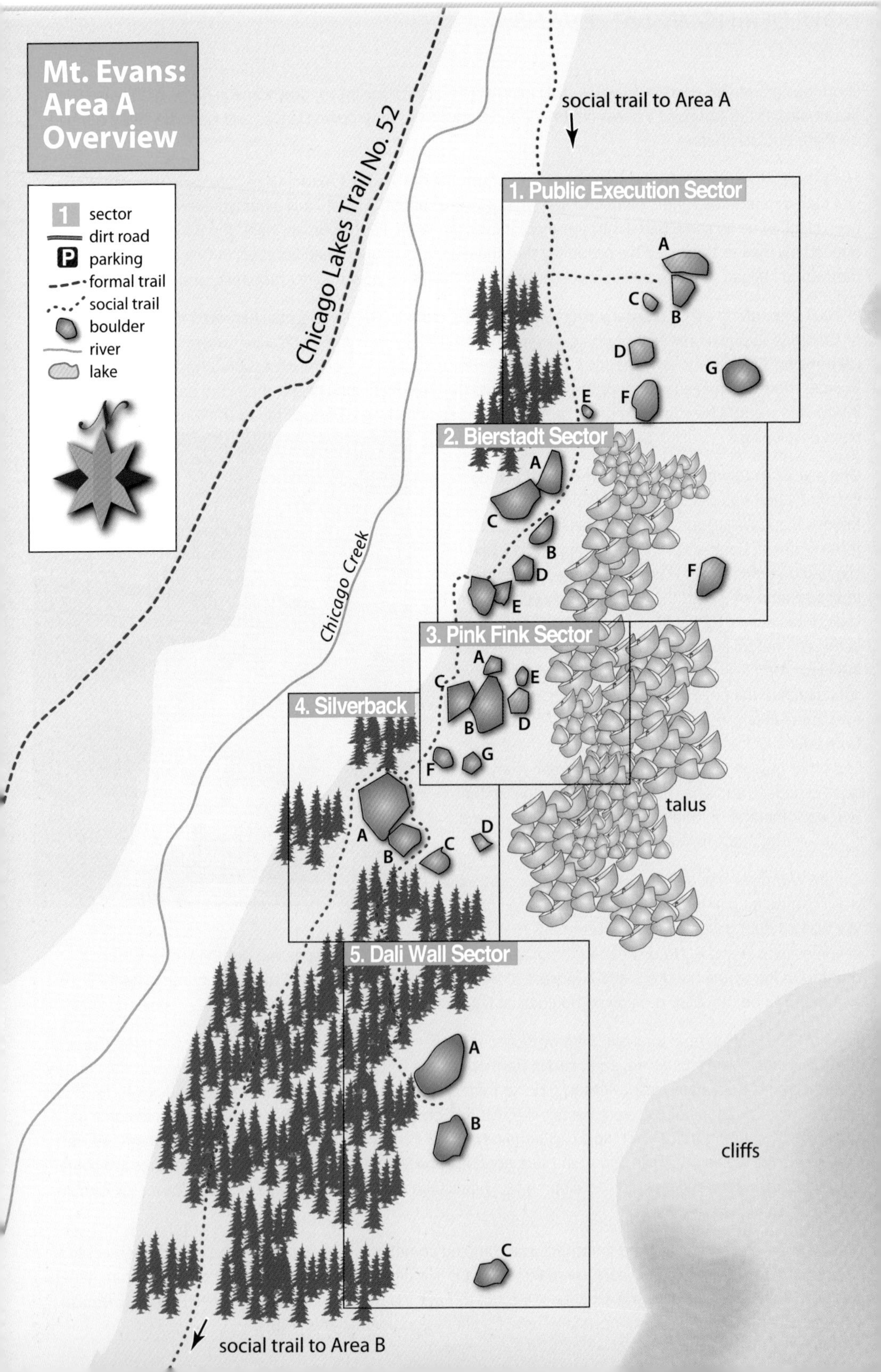
Mt. Evans: Area A Overview
1 sector
dirt road
P parking
formal trail
social trail
boulder
river
lake
Chicago Lakes Trail No. 52
Chicago Creek
social trail to Area A
1. Public Execution Sector
A
B
C
D
E
F
G
2. Bierstadt Sector
A
B
C
D
E
F
3. Pink Fink Sector
A
B
C
D
E
F
G
4. Silverback
A
B
C
D
talus
5. Dali Wall Sector
A
B
C
cliffs
social trail to Area B

Area A

Continue past The Gateway Boulder on the Chicago Lakes Trail No. 52. Beyond the meadow the trail leads up a small hill for 30 yds through some trees. The trail will flatten out and head slightly downhill. Look for an obvious social trail which heads left, 2.8 miles from Echo Lake. Follow this into the willows and cross Chicago Creek on two bridges constructed from logs. Most of the bouldering at Area A is around this now-well-worn social trail that skirts the edge of the talus field. It is 3.0 miles to Bierstadt (a classic V10) from the parking lot at Echo Lake. The elevation of Area A is around 11,040 ft.

Area A Approach

Public Execution Sector

After crossing the second log bridge, head right on the social trail through the woods. After 200 yds, turn left off the social trail at a small cairn and head up a faint trail 40 yds towards the cliffband. Sidewinder faces the approaching climber. For those wishing to continue on to the main sectors of Area A, continue on the social trail for another 100 yds to Beirstadt, on page 40.

A. Sidewinder Boulder

❒ 1. **Sidewinder V6** ★★
Stand start on a good sloping hold and traverse the lip from right to left.
FA Ben Scott 2003

❒ 2. **Jeremy's Traverse V8** ★★
Right of #1. Start matched on a flat rail just right of a small boulder. Traverse right.
FA Jeremy Bisher 2003

Sidewinder

Sidewinder Boulder-Bisher Traverse

Nic Oklobzija on Timeline V1

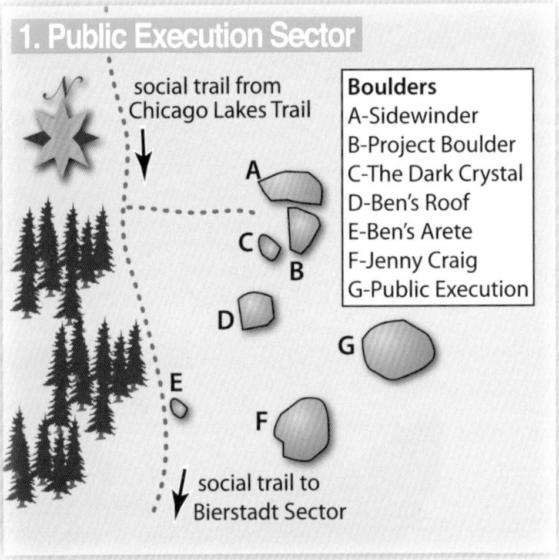

B. Project Boulder

Just right of Jeremy's Traverse is this nice face with two obvious and difficult projects.

❒ 1. **Project**
Climb the short and steep face on small sidepulls and crimps.

❒ 2. **Project**
Climb the obvious and colorful arête.

❒ 3. **V4** ★★
Around the corner from the Project Face on the same boulder. Start on a positive crimp. Climb straight up the wall.

C. The Dark Crystal

Downhill 5 yds from the Project Boulder.

❒ 1. **The Dark Crystal V3** ★★★
Start standing on a left-hand crystal pocket and a right-hand edge. Climb the slab.
FA Ben Scott 2002

Project Boulder

The Dark Crystal

D. Ben's Roof

Walk 15 yds upcanyon along the edge of the talus on a faint trail from The Dark Crystal to a small cluster of dense willows. This short problem faces away from the cilff.

❒ 1. **Ben's Roof V9** ★
Sit start with a left hand on a flat edge in the seam, right hand on a low, rounded sidepull. A Ben Scott classic.
FA Chuck Fryberger 2004

E. Ben's Arête

From Ben's Roof, walk upcanyon and away from the cliff 25 yds. This lies right off the social trail, about 280 yds from the second Chicago Creek crossing, on the left side of the trail.

❒ 1. **Ben's Arête V6** ★★
Start sitting, matched on a small, crimpy sidepull on the face. Pull on and slap up and right to the corner of the arête.
FA Ben Scott 2003

Ben's Arête

Ben's Roof

F. Jenny Craig Boulder

Continue on the social trail 10 yds beyond Ben's Arête and into a small clearing. Cut back uphill and left on a faint trail for 20 yds to these two problems.

❒ 1. **Jenny Craig V7** ★★
Start standing, on the left side of the slab, and traverse the feature to the right.
FA Chuck Fryberger 2004

Jenny Craig

G. Public Execution

Just uphill and to the left of Jenny Craig 10 yds.

❒ 1. **Public Execution V10** ★★★
Sit start on the left side, straddling the arête, and climb the seam traverse. Top out up the tall, right side.
FA James Litz 2004

Public Execution

Bierstadt Sector

From the cutoff up to Jenny Craig, continue on the social trail 25 yds to a couple of massive boulders. From the creek crossing on the social trail Bierstadt is about 300 yds.

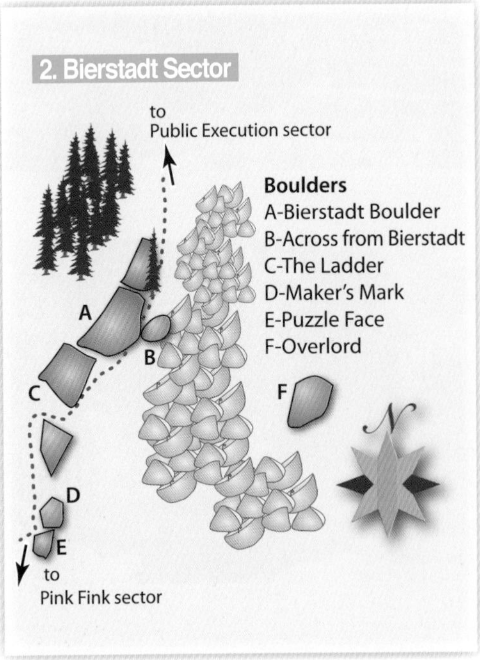

A. Bierstadt Boulder

❒ 1. **V8** ★★
Start sitting on edges just right of a pine tree and climb up hidden edges to a sketchy finish.
FA Greg Loomis 2004

❒ 2. **Project**
Traverse the wall on good flat edges from right to left and do some hard moves up the arête.

❒ 3. **Project**
Make a hug move up and right, then top out left.

❒ 4. **Ludders Pinch V6** ★★
Start standing, matched on a good edge. Climb up and left through a terrible sloper. Ludders Pinch Low starts on Bierstadt and climbs this to finish at V8.
FA Dave Ludders 2003

❒ 5. **Bierstadt V10** ★★★
Start standing on a low right-hand jug and a lower left hand sidepull. Climb up the compression feature. Classic and steep alpine granite. Taller climbers will find this to be more V9, shorter climbers V10.
FA Ben Scott 2003

Bierstadt Boulder

❒ 6. **Banksy V9** ★★
Start standing, four feet left of Bierstadt, on a right-hand pinch and a left-hand edge. Climb right, into Bierstadt.
FA Jamie Emerson 2009

Walk past Bierstadt and underneath the Bierstadt Arête. Timeline and Canvas are on the large open slab on the right.

❒ 7. **Bierstadt Arête V1** ★
Stand start and climb the arête.

❒ 8. **Timeline V1** ★★★
Stand start, climb up the slab and into the dihedral. The crux is the final move. Committing and excellent.
FA Ben Scott 2002

❒ 9. **Canvas V4** ★★
Climb the very tall and committing slab to the left. Sit start for full credit.
FA Ben Scott 2004

Bierstadt Boulder

Bierstadt Boulder-Timeline

B. Across From Bierstadt

❒ 1. **V1** ★★
Start standing, matched on a good edge.

❒ 2. **V3** ★★
Start standing, matched on a good edge and dyno up and left to a good edge.

❒ 3. **Sober Stoner V7** ★★
Start sitting on a left-facing flat hold and climb the non-descript face to the top.

Across From Bierstadt

C. The Ladder Boulder

Continue on the social trail, past Beirstadt on the right, and through the overhang. The Ladder Boulder touches the face just left of Canvas.

❒ 1. **Zorro V6** ★★
Start standing on good chest-high hold and climb the arête.
FA Ben Scott 2003

❒ 2. **Zorro Moderate V1** ★
Start sitting on a good flat edge. Climb up and left.

The Ladder Boulder-Zorro

❒ 3. **The Ladder V2** ★★★★
Just left of #2, on the other side of a small boulder. Start standing on a sloping edge. Climb straight up on good rock and classic moves. A lower start adds a couple of nice moves and a grade of difficulty.
FA Ben Scott 2001

❒ 4. **Traverse V5** ★★
Continue around the boulder to this short overhanging face. Start in the middle of the wall on a jug and traverse the wall left to right.

❒ 5. **Last of the Ohitians V2** ★★★
Walk left of Traverse to a long slab on the backside of the boulder, opposite The Ladder. Stand start and climb the delicate slab.
FA Doug McKee 2003

❒ 6. **Ground Control V11** ★★
Sit start on a low, rounded jug. Great rock, but difficult not to dab.
FA Chris Shulte 2007

The Ladder Boulder-The Ladder

The Ladder Boulder-Last of the Ohitians

The Ladder Boulder

The Ladder Boulder-Ground Control

Maker's Mark

D. Maker's Mark Boulder

❒ 1. **V4** ★★
Start standing on a good jug. Head up and right.
FA Ben Scott 2003

❒ 2. **Maker's Mark V5** ★★
Start standing on scuplted holds. Climb the overhang to a tricky mantel.
FA Dave Ludders 2003

❒ 3. **Maker's Mark Sit Start V8** ★★
Start on a left-hand edge and a low right-hand sidepull/undercling, and climb into Makers Mark.
FA Jade Whitney

Maker's Mark Boulder-V4

E. Puzzle Face

❒ 1. **Puzzle Arête V6** ★★
Start standing and climb the arête. Weird.
FA Ben Scott 2002

❒ 2. **Puzzle Face V4** ★★
Start high by stepping off the rock.
FA Ben Scott 2002

Maker's Mark

Puzzle Face

F. The Overlord

The Overlord is off the social trail, up in the massive pile of boulders. Facing The Ladder, turn around 180 degrees and walk around the chossy boulder opposite The Ladder, on the right side. Pick your way straight up the hillside 50 yds to this excellent boulder. Refer to the map on page 40.

❒ 1. **Crystal Seam V4** ★★
Start in a blocky layback and work through a short roof. Continue up the seam to the slab.
FA Ben Scott 2004

❒ 2. **Overlord V8** ★★★
A very technical beginning on thin holds leads to an undercling under the roof. Big compression climbing leads to a long move over the lip.
FA Ben Scott 2004

❒ 3. **Stylee Streaks V4** ★★★
Climb the obvious crimp rails to a big throw to the lip.
FA Ben Scott 2004

❒ 4. **Black Stain V2** ★
Match on a crimp rail and move up and right through the black streak.
FA Ben Scott 2004

The Overlord

Melissa Lacasse on Bierstadt V10 Photo by Andy Mann

Pink Fink Sector

From Puzzle Face, continue along the social trail with a low and long boulder on your left. Make a hard left around the corner of the boulder and continue through the dense willows. The trail will come out of the willows near Peasants into Leaders, on the left, and Pink Fink straight ahead. Walk left of Peasants into Leaders 10yds.

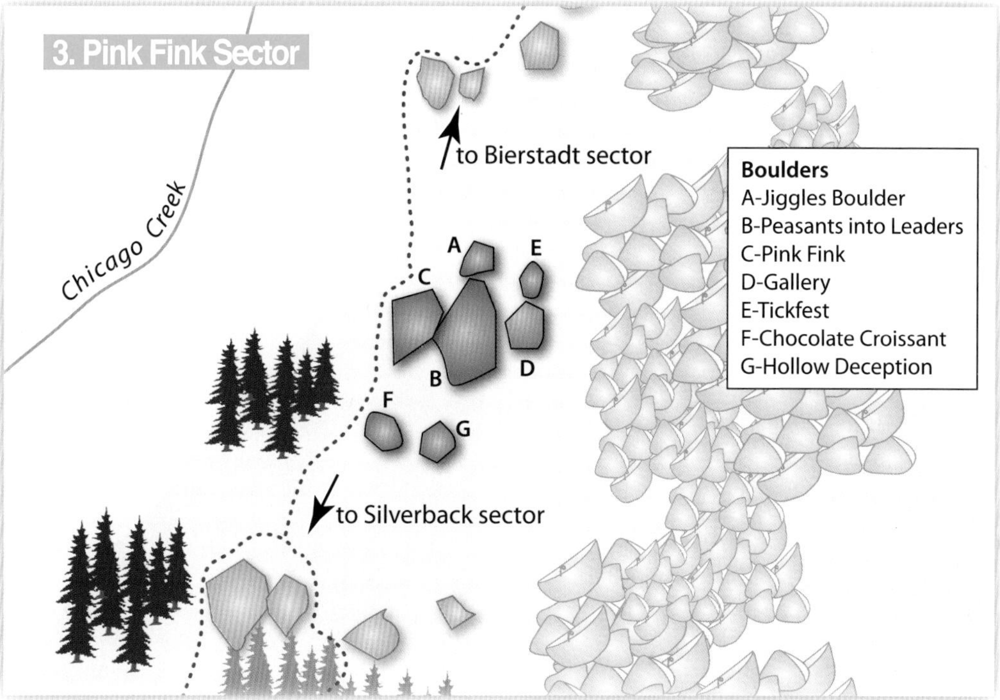

A. Jiggle Boulder

❒ 1. **Jiggle V8** ★★
Sit start on two edges, climb up and left to an interesting topout.
FA Charles Fryberger 2003

❒ 2. **Project**
Sit start on two edges, climb up and right. Contrived.

B. Peasants into Leaders Boulder

❒ 1. **Project**
Climb the left side of the overhanging face on the left side of the boulder from a low left-hand tooth.

❒ 2. **Black Crack V1** ★★
Stand start on a good edge. Work your way up the seam. Tall.
FA Ben Scott 2003

❒ 3. **Peasants into Leaders V7** ★★★★
Start matched on a good undercling. Climb straight up. One of the proudest problems in Colorado. This outstanding line went unclimbed for several years, until Ben Scott made a proud FA. A classic highball.
FA Ben Scott 2007

❒ 4. **V6** ★★
Ten feet right of Peasants into Leaders. Squeeze between boulders right of Peasants..., or walk around the Pink Fink Boulder. Start on a right-hand sidepull and a left-hand gaston. Make a big move up and left, then trend back right.
FA Ben Scott 2004

C. Pink Fink Boulder

Just right of the Peasants into Leaders Boulder.

❒ 1. **Highball Slab V3** ★★
Stat high, on a good blocky hold. The crux is up high, right where it should be.

❒ 2. **Pink Fink V6** ★★
Stand start left hand on a sloping gaston, right hand on an incut flake. This broke recently and may be harder.
FA Greg Loomis 2003

❒ 3. **Snow White V7** ★★
Start as for Pink Fink, but head left on sloping edges.
FA Pat Goodman 2003

❒ 4. **The Quill V7** ★
Facing Pink Fink, walk right around the boulder on the social trail to this short roof. Stand start on underclings.
FA Ben Scott 2003

Pink Fink-The Quill

D. The Gallery Boulder

Walk around the backside of the Peasants into Leaders Boulder, either by squeezing through boulders right of Peasants, or by walking around Pink Fink and past The Quill on the social trail. Head back over towards the Peasants into Leaders Boulder, hugging it around left. Crawl into a small corridor which opens up. The Gallery is in on the right.

❒ 1. **The Gallery V8** ★★
Sit start on a left sidepull and a right-hand gaston at the bottom of the obtuse dihedral. Climb the seam and head left to top out. A right exit goes at V7 and is also a Ben Scott first ascent.
FA Ben Scott 2003

Peasants into Leaders Boulder

Peasants into Leaders Boulder-V6

Pink Fink

E. Tickfest Boulder

The slab just left of The Gallery is the top of the Tickfest Boulder. Walk up the slab then jump down, off the boulder, and look left.

❒ 1. **Tickfest V6** ★★
Just behind The Gallery is a short face. Start sitting on a flat crimp edge down and left, and climb thin seams.

F. Chocolate Croissant

Continue on the social trail past The Quill for 15 yds, through a section that is often muddy. Chocolate Croissant is on the left side of the trail.

❒ 1. **Chocolate Croissant V5** ★★
Start standing with a right hand on a pinch, left hand on a sloper. Tricky, to say the least.
FA Greg Loomis 2004

G. Hollow Deception Boulder

Just behind Chocolate Croissant on the left is Hollow Deception.

❒ 1. **Hollow Deception V9** ★
Start standing on a left-hand incut that has broken several times (and continues to crumble) and a right hand low on another incut.

Silverback Sector

Continue 25 yds beyond Chocolate Croissant on the social trail to a massive boulder in the woods. Head right at the tree stump to go to Silverback, Chrome, and the path to Area B. Head left to visit Seurat, and the rest of the bouldering at Area A.

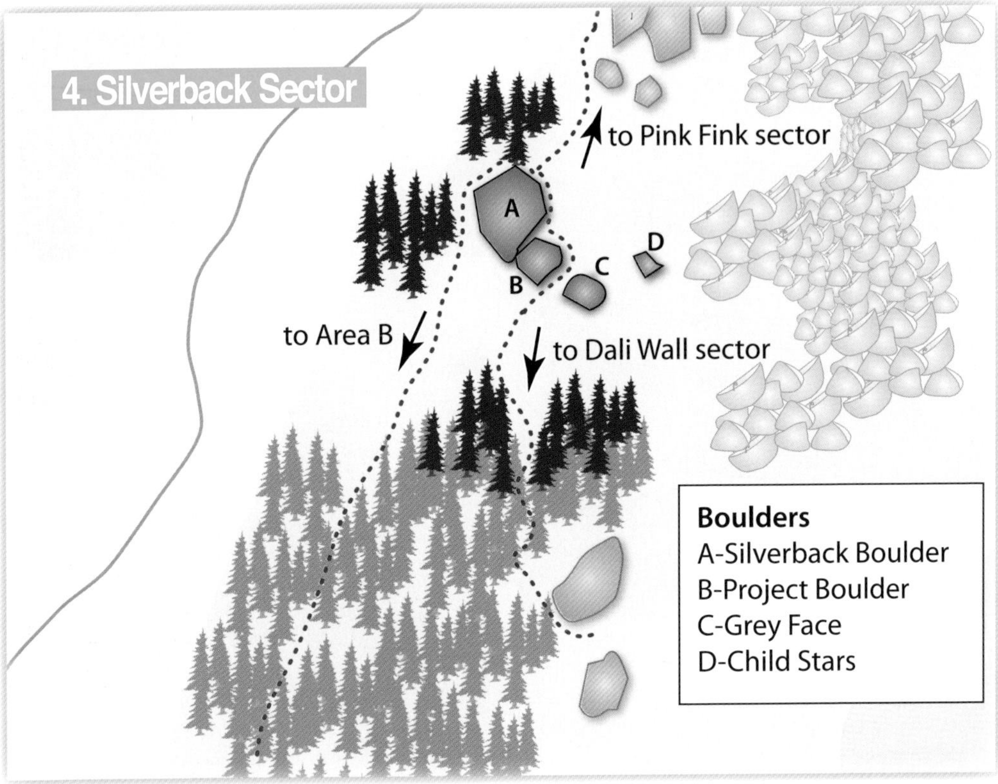

Seurat is a gorgeous testpiece at Area A. Here Ben Scott, the first ascentionist, demonstrates the proper starting holds. Ben named the problem after the famous pointillist painter Georges Seurat. Delicate liebacks and extremely poor feet make this problem a nightmare for many modern boulderers. The landing seems to get worse as one climbs higher and has claimed several ankles. In 2007, Lynn Hill flashed the problem, calling it 5.12.

Mt. Evans at sunset

A. Silverback Boulder

❒ 1. **Useless Tools V9**
Start matched on two flat edges. Hang straight down, with no feet, and campus up. Topout to the right.
FA James O'Connor 2009

❒ 2. **Blackie V11** ★
Stand start on two terrible pinches on the faint arête. Climb a couple difficult moves.
FA Tyler Landman 2007

❒ 3. **Broken Arrow V4** ★★
Start standing on high jugs. Climb up the seams. A difficult dyno was first climbed by Ben Scott by starting on Broken Arrow and jumping all the way to the lip.
FA Ben Scott 2003

❒ 4. **Seurat V8** ★★★
Start standing, with a right hand in the crack and a left hand palming on the face left of the crack. Climb the crack. Loved and hated. Classic.
FA Ben Scott 2003

❒ 5. **Project**
Climb the blunt prow over a poor landing.

❒ 6. **All Dogs Go To Evans V10** ★★
Start low on a crystal pinch. Traverse the thin lip to a slot hold under the roof. Continue traversing the lip, up and left through another hard section.
FA Clayton Reagan

❒ 7. **Rawhide V7** ★★
Start low on a crystal pinch. Traverse the thin lip to a hold under the roof, then bust a tough mantel and climb the tenuous and tall slab.

❒ 8. **Silverback V10** ★★★
Start standing on two slopers at 6 ft. Climb up the overhanging sloping feature. This problem is very condition dependent and what can feel impossible in the summer may feel almost easy in the freezing cold. Has been called V8–V11. A classic technical testpiece.
FA Randy Puro 2006

❒ 9. **Chrome V12** ★★★
Start sitting on a left-hand sidepull jug, at the bottom of a crack. Climb into Silverback.
FA Seth Allred 2007

B. Project Boulder

❒ 1. **Project**
Climb the clean face left of Seurat.

Famed European coursesetter Manu Hassler takes a break from setting the World Cup to send Silverback V10.

C. Grey Face Boulder

Facing Seurat, walk left around the Project Boulder on the social trail. This boulder is immediately on your left. Continue straight up the hill around the left side of the boulder to visit Child Stars, where this branch off of the main social trail will dead end. The Grey Face is on the opposite side from the Moderate.

❒ 1. **Grey Face Moderate V1** ★★
Start standing on good holds and climb straight up the feature.

❒ 2. **Grey Face V2** ★★
Start standing on crimps and make a big move up and right to a good flat edge. Climb straight up.

D. Child Stars Boulder

❒ 1. **Child Stars V12** ★★
Start sitting, matched on low incut underclings. Power out the roof.
FA Chris Schulte 2007

Grey Face Boulder-Moderate

Grey Face Boulder- Grey Face

Child Stars Boulder

The Dali Wall Sector

From Seurat, continue on the social trail, passing the Project Boulder on your right, and the Grey Face Moderate on your left. The trail heads uphill for 75 yds, crossing a large log half way. The Dali Boulder will appear on your left. (See map page 54.)

The Dali Boulder

A. The Dali Boulder

❒ 1. **Pat's Arête V7** ★★
Stand start on a large ledge and climb the arête.
FA Pat Goodman 2003

❒ 2. **Ode to the Modern Man V14** ★★★
Start standing on a left hand sloping sidepull and a small right hand sidepull. Three very hard moves lead to large sloping rail. Head left and finish with another difficult sequence on heel hooks, a bad pinch and a long lockoff.
FA Daniel Woods 2006

❒ 3. **Super Gui V11** ★★
Start on The Dali, dyno to the rail, and finish out left.
FA Clayton Reagan 2005

❒ 4. **The Dali V8** ★★★
Start sitting with a right hand on a left facing gaston and a left hand on a small crimp. Climb up, dyno, and finish out right. The second ascent, by Jamie Emerson, was done from a match on the lowest left facing gaston.
FA Ben Scott 2003

❒ 5. **Dali Crack V1**
Start sitting and climb the crack.

The Dali Boulder-Pat's Arête

The Dali Boulder

❒ 6. **Clear Blue Skies V11** ★★
Start sitting, matched on a low edge. The ultimate crimp ladder. One grade less than No More Greener Grasses.
FA Harry Robertson 2004

❒ 7. **Mental Pollution Low V12** ★
Start sitting, matched on a low edge. Head right, into Mental Pollution. Low in the grade.
FA Harry Robertson 2004

❒ 8. **Mental Pollution V10** ★
Start squatting, left hand on a sidepull edge, right hand on a very small sidepull. Make a big move up and right to a sloping crimp, then punch it to the friendliest jug in Colorado.
FA James Litz 2003

❒ 9. **No More Greener Grasses V12** ★★★★
Sit start on a flat jug with incuts. Climb straight up the wall. Amazing and difficult. Formerly known as "The Lime Wall Project." Perhaps the best of its grade in Colorado.
FA Luke Parady 2004

❒ 10. **Project**
Climb the arête.

❒ 11. **Goodman Face V3** ★★
Around the right side of The Dali Wall proper is this massive face. Climb straight up the featured edifice. The first ascent was done with no pre-inspection, onsight.
FA Pat Goodman 2003

❒ 12. **Project**
Continue around to the backside of the boulder to a looming overhanging wall. This project attempts to climb directly up the middle. Bold to say the least. Ben Scott stuck the huge move up to the right-facing flake a couple of times, but never finished this terrifying line.

❒ 13. **Serpentine Arête V6** ★★
Start at the base of the arête on crimps. Move out to the arête then climb it to a good hold and rockover.
FA Ben Scott 2004

Goodman Face

The Dali Boulder-Backside

B. Puddle Jumper

Just uphill 10 yds from The Dali Boulder is this welcoming boulder. A nice place to warm up, with relatively flat landings.

❒ 1. **Puddle Jumper V3** ★★★
Start standing and climb the crimpy slab. A great move.
FA Ben Scott 2003

❒ 2. **Nemesis V1** ★★
Climb the featured arête.

❒ 3. **Little Something for the Effort V2** ★★
Start on the arête, and head right onto the face.

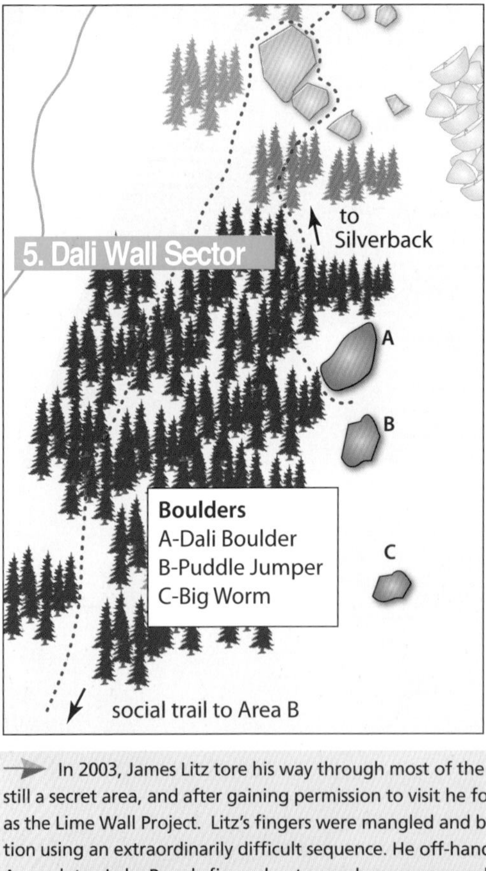

C. Big Worm

Walk around the right side of the Puddle Jumper Boulder and walk towards the cliffband. Just beyond a lone pine tree, 30 yds from The Dali Boulder and down in a hole is Big Worm.

❒ 1. **Big Worm V14** ★★
Start at the bottom of the hole, on a left-hand pinch and right hand on the arête. A very unique problem on great rock, but the enclosed nature of the climbing detracts from the quality. The stand start is Mirrormask V10.
FA Dave Graham 2009

In 2003, James Litz tore his way through most of the hardest problems in Colorado. At the time Mt. Evans was still a secret area, and after gaining permission to visit he found himself at the base of a gorgeous wave of rock known as the Lime Wall Project. Litz's fingers were mangled and bloody, but he managed to do the moves on the bottom section using an extraordinarily difficult sequence. He off-handedly remarked that he thought the full line could be V15. A year later, Luke Parady figured out a much more reasonable sequence, using a difficult shoulder move. He marched up to Mt. Evans alone, set his video camera on a tripod, and climbed the first ascent of one of the best problems in Colorado. Angela Payne made the FFA in 2010. Here Brian Capps works into the notorious shoulder move.
Photo by Hayden Miller.

Area B

Area B is a beautiful collection of quiet boulders near the treeline. The views towards the summit of Mt. Evans are sublime. This is still a somewhat developing area but good rock, a gorgeous setting and lack of visitors make it a wonderful destination. Facing Silverback, head right, around the boulder and pick up a good social trail that heads through the woods, upcanyon. Follow the social trail for about 600 yds (0.35 miles) or 7–10 minutes (depending on how fast you hike) to Random Progression which will appear on your left, 7 yds off the trail. The elevation of Area B is 11,279 ft.

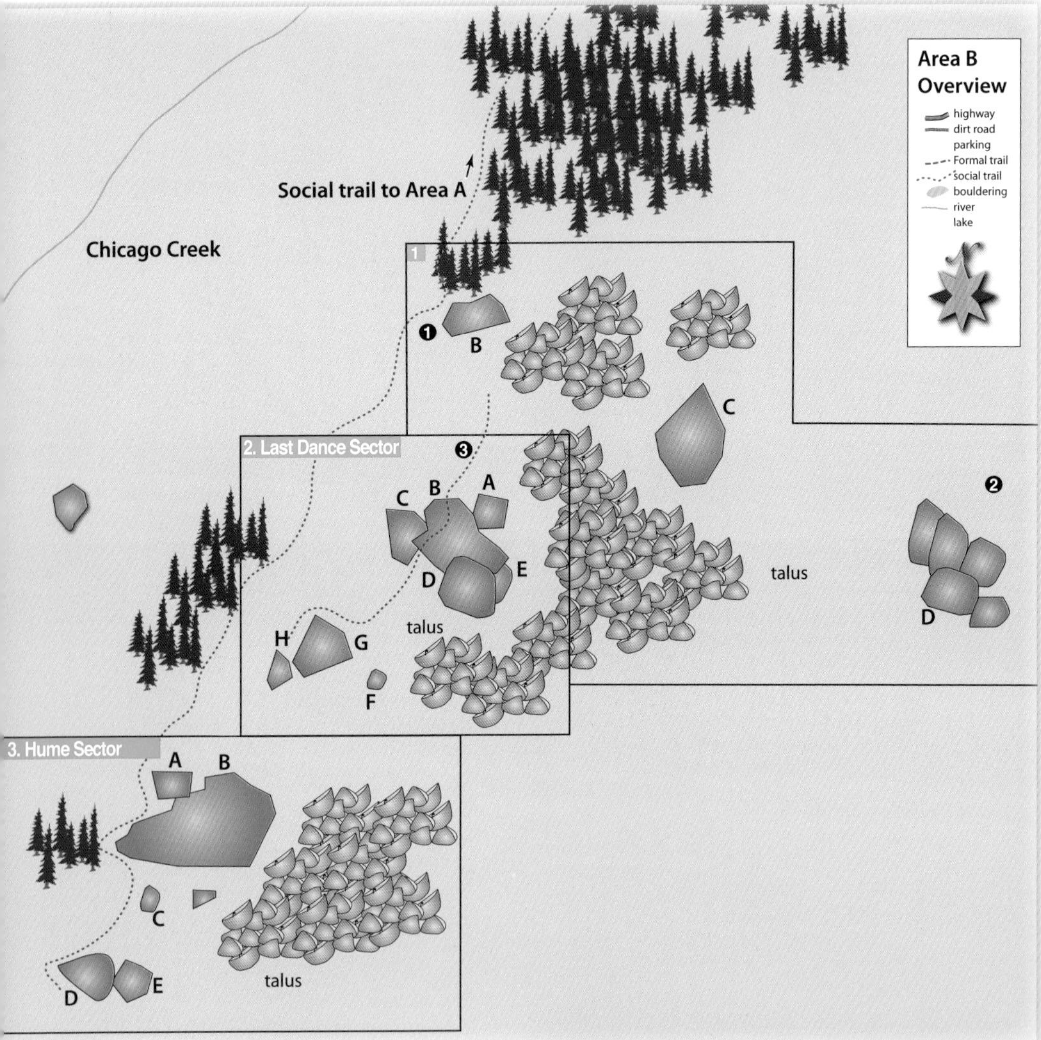

Gorillas in the Mist Sector

A. Random Progression

❒ 1. **Random Progression V7** ★★

Jump start to a sloping ball in the middle of the face.

FA Ben Scott 2004

B. Gorillas in the Mist

Continue on the trail another 325 yds (about three minutes) upcanyon from Random Progression. A massive talus field will appear on your left. Just beyond, step over a couple of crisscrossed, fallen logs and head up and left, off the social trail. Gorillas in the Mist is on a large boulder at the edge of the massive pile of rock. It faces the trail, about 10 yds off the trail on the left, on the right side of a long roof nearly devoid of features.

❒ 1. **Gorillas in the Mist V10** ★★★
Start matched on a good undercling and slap up awesome slopers and pinches. A great and unique feature, one of the best compression problems in Colorado. Originally suggested to be V8.
FA Cameron Cross 2004

Gorillas in the Mist

The B Seam

C. The B Seam

From Gorillas in the Mist, head around the boulder to the right and then straight up the hill about 100 yds. The bushes here can be dense and the talus is big and difficult to negotiate.

❒ 1. **The B Seam V4** ★★★
Start matched on a jug on the right side of the face and traverse the seam. An incredible problem, especially for the grade.

D. Sunseeker

Sunseeker is a long trudge up the hill, but well worth the effort. This is one of the best problems of its grade in the world. Hike uphill from The B Seam 200 yds to another cluster of large boulders high on the hill. Walk around the left side of the cluster before angling back right, as shown in the photo above. Walk around the overhanging boulder on the right, and the giant room will open up, down and right. Sunseeker faces uphill.

❒ 1. **Sunseeker V13** ★★★★
Start on a good rounded jug and climb up the amazing feature in the middle of the wall. This problem became public knowledge after a blog post on b3bouldering.com and was climbed a few days later by a visiting Finnish climber. An incredible line, with near-perfect rock. A very bold endeavor.
FA Nalle Hukkataival 2009

❒ 2. **Conspicuous Consumption V10** ★★★
Start matched on a high jug and climb the upper section.
FA Cameron Cross 2007

→ Carlo Traversi takes advantage of early season conditions to make the second ascent of Sunseeker V13. Photo by Andy Mann

LAST DANCE SECTOR

Head around the right side of Gorillas in the Mist on a faint trail through the willows. The obvious feature here is The Flake Boulder, which is a large visor of rock. Hike through the willows and over the talus for 75 yds.

A. LAST DANCE

Last Dance is just before The Flake Boulder on the left.

❒ 1. **Last Dance V7** ★★★
Start on a good jug and climb up the middle of the wall. Committing.
FA Jason Kehl 2007

B. THE FLAKE BOULDER

❒ 1. **Steiner im Flug V5** ★★
Start on the far left arête, down in the hole. Climb up then right out of this outrageous feature. Climb right to the far end of the flake.
FA Matt Battaglia

C. SAM HALL

On the boulder just below Steiner im Flug is this short overhang.

❒ 1. **Sam Hall V9** ★★
Start stitting, low on a good hold. Climb the short overhang.
FA Chris Schulte 2008

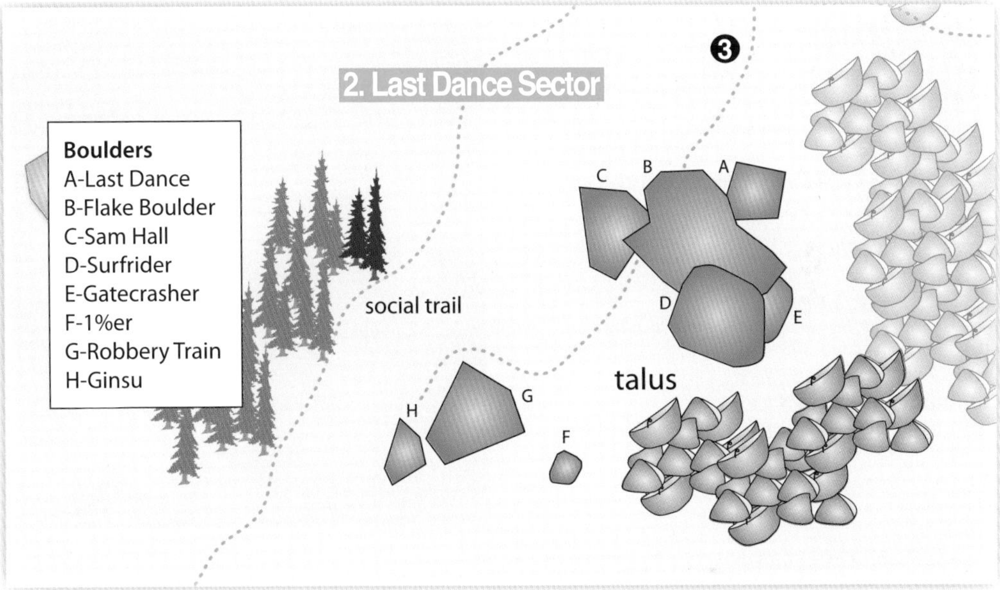

D. Surfrider Boulder

A prominent gray boulder, just uphill from the Flake Traverse.

❒ 1. **Surfrider V9** ★★

Start sitting on the right side of the face closest to the Flake Traverse, over the huge hole on the left. Climb up and left on edges. *FA Chris Schulte*

E. Gatecrasher Boulder

From Surfrider, head down into the cave to the left.

❐ 1. **Gatecrasher V12** ★★
Start sitting on a right hand-pinch and a small left hand. Move up and left to a sloper, then head right, out the hole and around the corner, and finish up to the right-trending crack. A tricky slab finish.
FA Chris Schulte

❐ 2. **V12** ★★
Start sitting on a right hand pinch and a small left hand. Move up and left to a sloper, then head left, up a nice compression feature and a sloping topout.
FA Chris Schulte

F. 1%er

Look back up the hill from Robbery Train.

❐ 1. **1%er V13** ★★★
Start standing on a right-hand jug sidepull, and a left-hand sloping edge. Do a few hard compression moves over a flat landing.
FA Chris Schulte 2010

G. Robbery Train

A massive boulder, 50 yds upcanyon from Flake Traverse. The crack faces uphill, towards the massive broken cliff towering overhead.

❐ 1. **Robbery Train V9** ★★★
Start standing with a good, left-facing hold in the crack.
FA Cameron Cross 2004

Justin Jaeger takes a lap on The B-Seam Photo: by Sockhands Collection

H. Ginsu

❒ 1. **Ginsu V9** ★★★

Start standing with a rounded edge for the left hand on the right side of the face, and right-hand undercling. Make a big move up and right.

FA Ben Scott 2003

❒ 2. **Ginsu Sit V11** ★★

Start sitting very low, move to a right-hand sidepull and climb a few moves into the stand start.

FA Chris Schulte 2009

Hume Sector

From Gorillas in the Mist, continue along the social trail through the willows 175 yds to a clearing. The Crystal Face will appear in a clearing on your left.

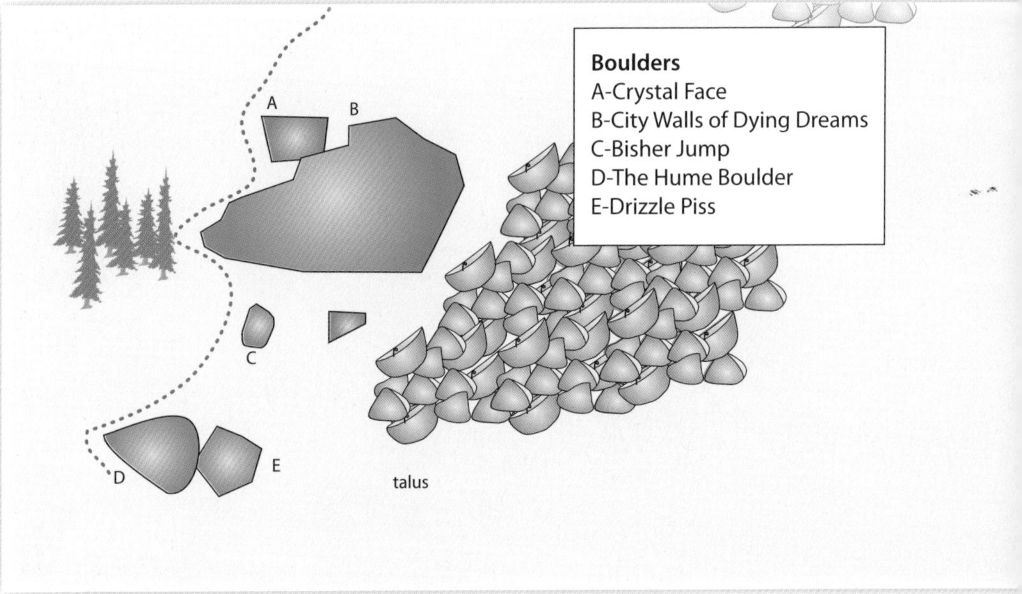

A. Crystal Face

The trail will open up right at the Crystal Face, on the left.

❒ 1. **Crystal Arête V3** ★★

Start standing and climb the arête.

❒ 2. **Crystal Face V5** ★★

Climb the middle of the face to a scary move up high.

B. City Walls of Dying Dreams

Walk around the Crystal Face and look left to the prominent arête.

❒ 1. **City Walls of Dying Dreams V10** ★★★

An absolutely stunning arête. Start standing and climb technical and difficult moves over a poor landing. Adam Osterhoff climbed the sit start first at V11. The top is difficult, and has claimed a broken leg.

FA Cameron Cross 2005

Flannery Shay-Nemirow

"The secret of this kind of climbing," said Japhy, "is like Zen. Don't think. Just dance along. It's the easiest thing in the world, actually easier than walking on flat ground which is monotonous. The cute little problems present themselves at each step and yet you never hesitate and you find yourself on some other boulder you picked out for no special reason at all, just like Zen."
-Jack Kerouac, The Dharma Bums

Though Jack Kerouac is speaking about the joys of talus hopping, it's hard not to associate the language and the feeling with alpine bouldering. It's the monotony of the flat land that drives us into the mountains, in search of some boulder that we obsess over for no particular reason. Kerouac is not a climber but he understands the mindful experience. At some point, it is best to turn off your mind, to stop questioning (though it is the nature of this beast, to question) and accept that you're on this boulder for no special reason, except that at some point, you wanted to be there. That is enough, to want to be there, to want to fall and fail, and eventually succeed, in one of the most stunning places on earth.

Going to Mt. Evans is an adventure, going to the Park is exciting. To hike is a slog, until you remember how unique it is. To climb is a chore, until you realize how much fun it is to sit around with friends while trying harder than you ever thought possible. To fall is frustrating until you find yourself on top of a boulder. I find myself going through almost every possible combination of these feelings every time I go up into the alpine zone. Contradictory feelings or not, Area A is a great change from ennui of gym climbing. Frustration or not, Lower Chaos is a refreshing break from work or school. Without the mountains we would lack a sense of perspective so important to our sanity. The towering peaks and fragile tundra justify the frustration that shadows climbing. Sunsets. Wildlife. Flowers. Landscapes bordering on sublime. This is what sets apart the bouldering at Mt. Evans and Rocky Mountain National Park from the likes of Flagstaff Mountain and Morrison.

I suspect you'll agree when I say that climbing is interesting. There is something deeply engaging about it, the intricacies seen in a single foot movement, or the most effective way to take a hand hold. But these are all details one could see in gym climbing; it's the unknowable nature of the mountains that makes the activity especially compelling. There are so many variables, so many uncontrolled facets of alpine bouldering that it makes any dogmatic approach impossible. The weather may refuse to cooperate or the sun could be in just the wrong place for the last throw to the lip. But when the climbing is good, it's great, and when it's bad you're still lucky to experience the majesty of the alpine experience.

Jason Kehl on the first ascent of Last Dance V7. Photo by Andy Mann

C. Bisher Jump

Head right instead of left, around the City Walls of Dying Dreams Boulder and away from the problem itself. The Bisher Jump is 15 yds away, on a separate boulder, and faces downhill, towards Chicago Creek.

❒ 1. **Bisher Jump V8** ★★
Stack some pads and jump start to the high sloper. Follow the seam to a high finish.
FA Jeremy Bisher 2004

D. The Hume Boulder

Look right from the Bisher Jump and walk 25 yds to the obvious overhanging face, down a small hill and back up again.

❒ 1. **The Dreamtime Project**
This obvious and amazing project has yet to be climbed. Will be best and hardest from down low.

❒ 2. **Curiously Wrong V7** ★★
Walk around the right side of the boulder 15 yds. Start crouched on a crimp edge. Move up left to a broken edge, match, then finish with a big move out left to a jug.

❒ 3. **Curiously Strong V8** ★★
Start crouched on a crimp edge. Move up left to a broken edge, match, then finish with a huge move straight up to the top of the wall.

❒ 4. **Mind of a Gold Fish V4** ★★
Start on a rounded edge. Move left to a good gaston.

❒ 5. **Hume Problem V9** ★★★
Start sitting on one pad, matched on a very poor undercling. Dave Hume made the first ascent in a driving rainstrom. Great moves on good rock, and a very hard start.
FA David Hume 2004

E. Drizzle Piss

Just around the corner from the Hume Problem, this problem is on the adjacent, uphill boulder. Walk right, around a tall and easy slab. This excellent highball faces uphill, towards the cliffband.

❒ 1. **Drizzle Piss V7** ★★★
Stand start on good edges in the middle of the face. Climb good edges straight up the middle. A committing move up high.
FA Ben Scott 2004

Also, two recent additions of note: The first is a big block arête with a bad slab landing called One False Move V4. The second is right of that, just before you turn the corner for Bisher Jump. It is a yellow lichened wall called White Lightning V8. Start on the face and climb up until you can throw out right for the arête. These lines were established by Jason Kehl.

Drizzle Piss

The Hume Boulder-Dreamtime Project

The Hume Boulder-Curiously Strong

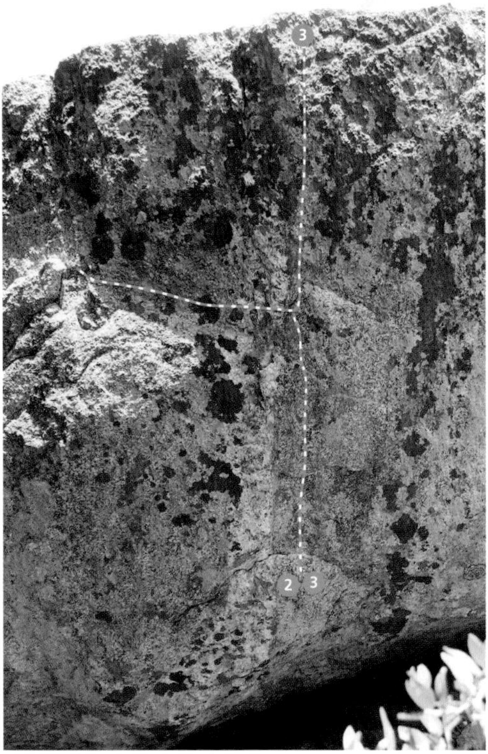

The Hume Boulder

Laying in Wait Sector

From Interstate 70 take the Idaho Springs exit #240. Head south on CO Highway 103 (a Scenic Byway) for 6.9 miles. Turn right on West Chicago Creek Road (a dirt road). Drive 2.9 miles to a parking area for Hells Hole Trailhead. The boulder sits on the north side of the dirt road directly across from the parking area's Do Not Enter sign, and is easily visible.

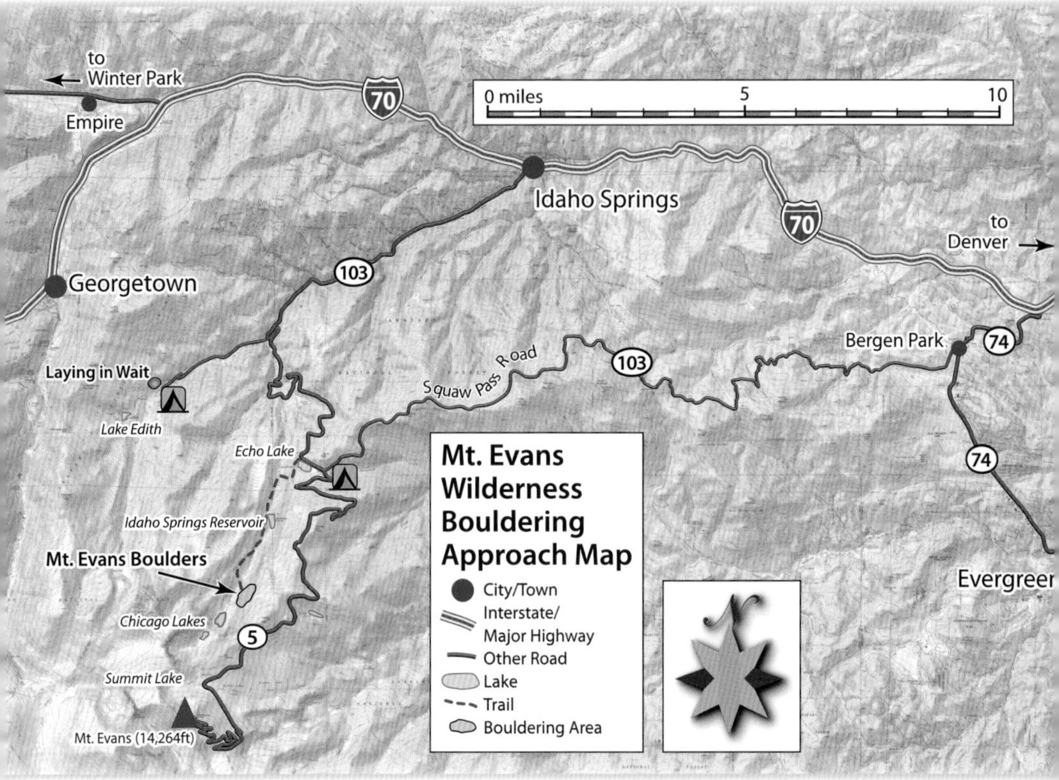

Laying in Wait

❒ 1. **Laying in Wait V8** ★★★★
Start on the far left side and climb up and right. One of the best and hardest slabs in the state. Chris Schulte has climbed a contrived line straight up the middle of the face at V9.
FA Ben Scott 2004

❒ 2. **V1** ★★★
The far right side of the block has a couple of variations to warm up on.

Laying in Wait

Part 2 Rocky Mountain National Park

Daniel Woods on Don't Get too Greedy V13. Photo by Steve Woods

Rocky Mountain National Park (RMNP)

Rocky Mountain National Park is located in northern Colorado, just outside Estes Park. It is more than 265,770 acres of mountainous terrain. More than 3 million people visit "the Park" every year. It is home to the headwaters of the Colorado River and to Trail Ridge Road, the highest paved thru highway in the country. There are more than 350 miles of hiking trails in RMNP. The Park contains 150 lakes and 450 miles of streams and rivers. Longs Peak is the highest point at 14,259 ft, which makes it one of the 54 peaks in Colorado taller than 14,000 ft. It is the only mountain in the Park over 14,000 ft.

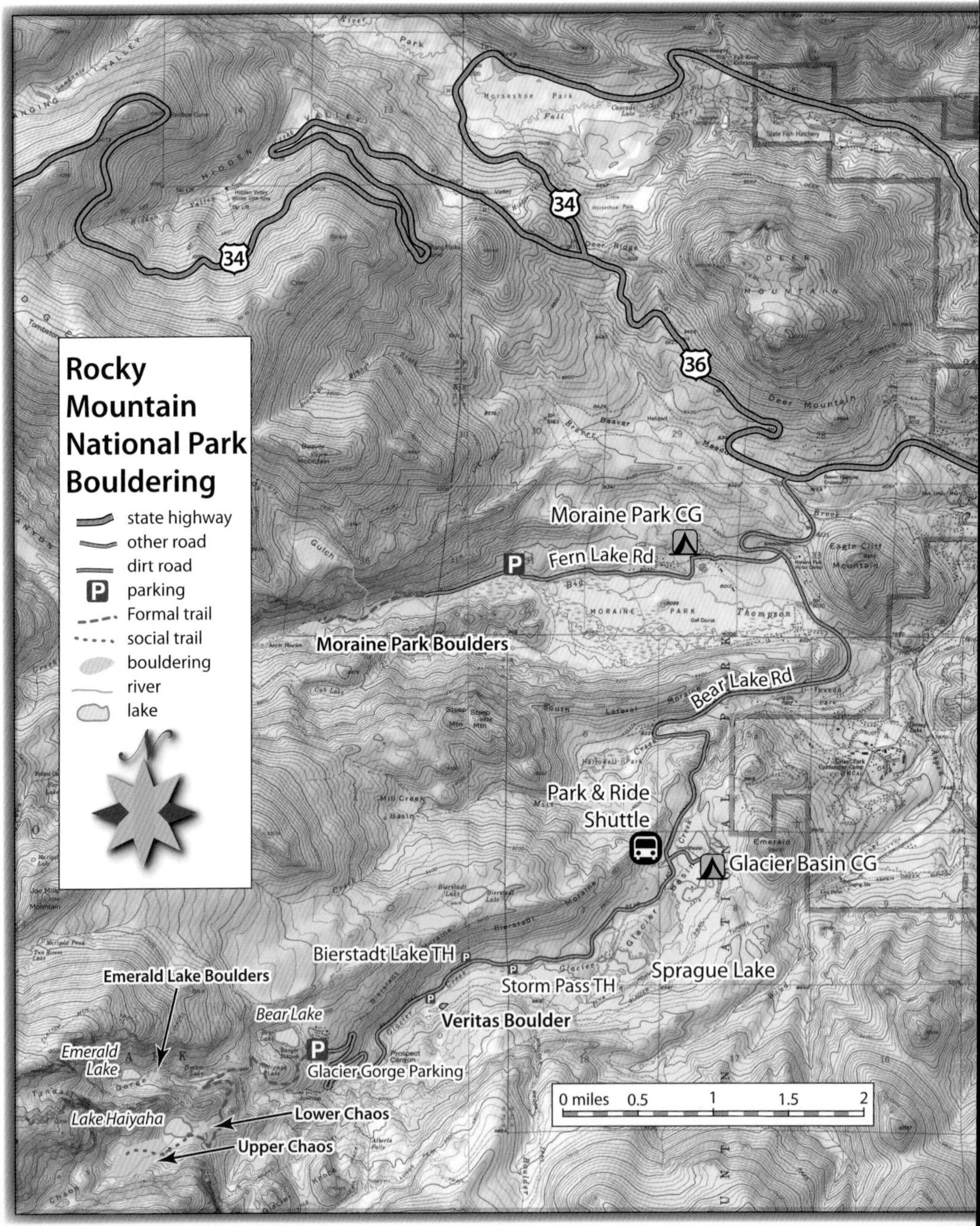

Getting There

Climbers visiting internationally should use Denver International Airport (DIA). From DIA head west on Pena Blvd for 3.5 miles. Take E-470 (which is a toll road) for 17.5 miles to I-25. (For those not wishing to pay the toll continue on Pena Blvd to I-70 W. Take this for 6 miles to I-270. Follow this to I-25 N to the junction with E-470). Take I-25 north for 15.5 miles to Hwy 66. Exit and head west on Hwy 66 for 15.7 miles. Hwy 66 turns into Hwy 36, and take this for 20.3 miles to Estes Park.

From Denver take Hwy 36 W out of the city and through Boulder. 14.8 miles outside of Boulder, turn left at the light, remaining on Hwy 36 W. Follow signs through Lyons and remain on Hwy 36 W for 20.3 miles to Estes Park. RMNP is 71 miles from downtown Denver.

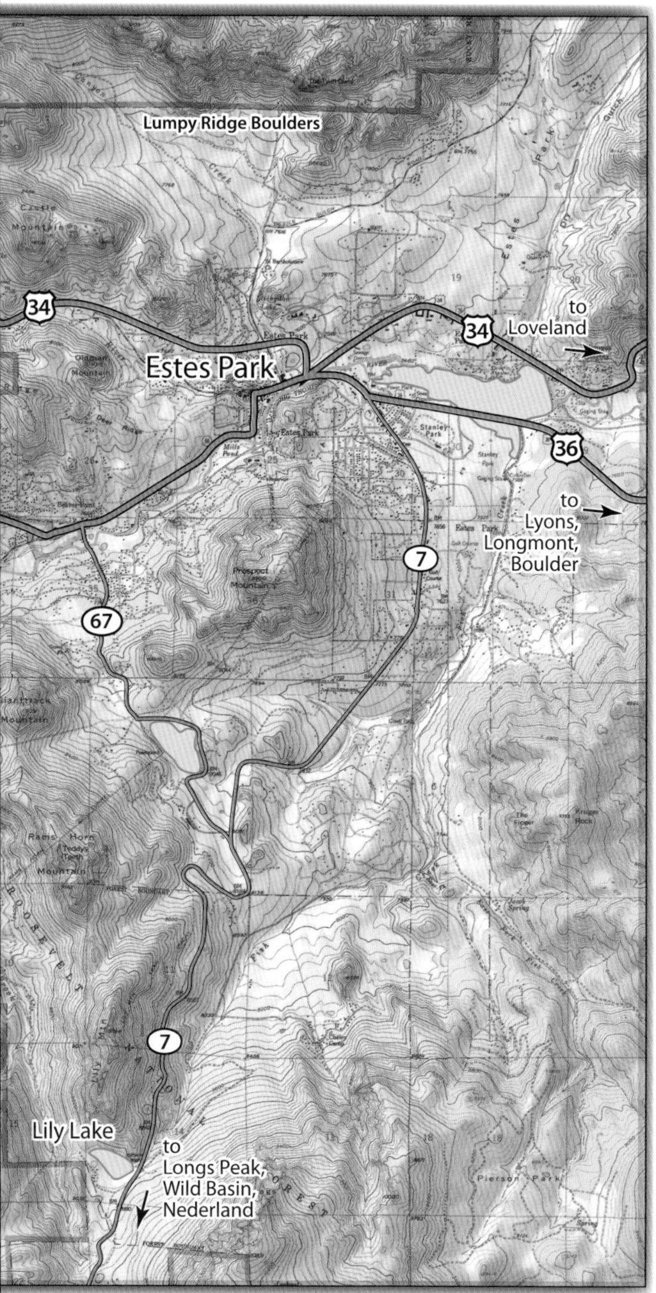

From Ft. Collins, take I-25 South to Hwy 34. Head west on Hwy 34 for 27.5 miles to Estes Park. In Estes Park Hwy 34 heads right at the first stop light. Go straight through the light on Hwy 36. Ft. Collins is 43 miles from RMNP. Follow signs to RMNP and stay on Hwy 36 through Estes Park. If coming from Denver or Boulder, turn left onto Big Thompson Ave (Hwy 36 W). Pass a pedestrian stoplight. Go straight at the next light, and turn left on Moraine Ave (Hwy 36 W) in downtown. Get in the right lane, crest a small hill, and veer right, staying on Hwy 36 W, following signs to RMNP. On the outskirts of town, pass the Country Market on the left. Go through a final stoplight and continue straight on Hwy 36. The road will bend to the right. Pass the Rocky Mountain National Park Entrance sign on the right and, soon after, the Beaver Meadows Visitor Center on the left. The Beaver Meadows Entrance to RMNP is 1.1 miles from here.

RMNP Accommodations

Estes Park is the jumping off point for most everyone entering the Park from the east. It is a tourist town with a population of about 6,000 people. It sits at an elevation of 7,522 ft. The hectic tourist season runs from Memorial Day until Labor Day, although weekends in September can be extremely busy as well. There are many hotels in Estes Park, and visitors should expect to have reservations in the summer months and to pay over $100 a night.

Camping

For many climbers on a limited budget, hotels are simply not an option. For the climber looking to camp, there are private pay-campgrounds in Estes Park. Rates vary from $20 to $60 a night, depending on your vehicle, the season, and your desired level of comfort.

For climbers looking to camp within RMNP (closer to the boulders than Estes Park) there are five pay-campgrounds, with a total of 586 campsites. This is the cheapest option for those looking to stay in the area. The maximum stay allowed is seven nights from June 1–Sept 30 and 14 nights from Oct 1–May 31. The campgrounds closest to the bouldering are Aspenglen, Glacier Basin, and Moraine Park. Campsites are $20 a night. Reservations can be made up to six months in advance by calling 888.448.1474.

Camping in the Park is a good option for those wishing to wake up every morning in the midst of the mountains.

Glacier Basin has 150 sites, is the closest campground to the bouldering, and is open from mid May until the first week of September.

Aspenglen has 54 sites, is the site furthest from the bouldering, and is open from mid-May until the end of September.

Moraine Park has 245 sites, is the second-closest site from most of the bouldering, and is open from the end of May to the beginning of October

www.nps.gov/romo/planyourvisit/camping.htm is a great source for more information on RMNP.

For those who don't mind making the hour or so drive (depending on the tourist traffic) every climbing day, the best option is to find a friend in Boulder or Fort Collins and crash on their couch. There is no free camping in Estes Park or Boulder.

Estes Park in the fall, looking towards RMNP and the Continental Divide

Food

There are plenty of places to grab a bite to eat before or after a long day in the mountains. Here are some of the most popular:

Ed's Cantina: Ed's provides cheap food in a climber-friendly atmosphere. A step above the McDonalds just down the road. 390 East Elkhorn Ave, 970.586.2919, www.edscantina.com

Rock Inn: A climber favorite. Great food at a fairly reasonable price. Many gluten-free and vegetarian dishes. 1675 Hwy 66, Estes Park, CO, 970.586.4116, www.rockinestes.com

The Dunraven Inn Restaurant: Excellent food and wine, but not inexpensive. A great place to go celebrate when you've sent your project. 2470 Hwy 66, Estes Park, CO, 970.586.6409, www.dunraveninn.com

Kind Coffee: Good coffee and wireless internet. 470 E. Elkhorn Ave, Estes Park, CO, 970.586.5206, www.kindcoffee.com

Stanley Hotel: The Stanley Hotel is the conspicuous white building on the north side of town. It's a great place for cocktails after climbing, and provides somewhat luxurious accomodations for those without a budget. 333 Wonderview Ave, Estes Park, CO 80517 800.976.1377, www.stanleyhotel.com

For more visitor Information on all of what Estes Park has to offer visit www.estes-park.com/

Things to do / Rest Days

Trail Ridge Road Scenic Drive: One of the most outstanding non-natural features of RMNP is Trail Ridge Road. It is a designated scenic byway, and it traverses 54 miles of RMNP from Estes Park to Grand Lake, CO at a maximum elevation of 12,183 ft. There are numerous pullouts to stop and enjoy the incredible vistas and sweeping views of the Continental Divide. It is closed all winter and opens and closes, depending on the weather, sometime in late May and early October.

Hiking: RMNP is world-renowned for its incredible scenery and there is no better way to experience it than to go for a hike. The Glacier Gorge Trailhead is a great place to start, although the small lot can fill up quickly in the summer. The Loch, Black Lake, Andrews Glacier and Alberta Falls all make great destinations. The Bear Lake Trailhead is another great starting point and is also the parking for most of the bouldering in RMNP. For those interested in solitude, Wild Basin provides long hikes with plenty of quiet space and astounding vistas. A rest-day hike will rarely disappoint, and the potential to find new rock is a powerful motivator. For those interested in solitude, the Indian Peaks Wilderness, just south of RMNP, is a great place to visit. The scenery is spectacular and there are boulders out there hiding in the woods. Head south from Estes Park on Hwy 7, the Peak to Peak Hwy. This is a scenic drive, and there are several trailheads along the way, most notably Brainard Lake.

Climbing: RMNP is also world-renowned for its alpine rock climbing. There are hundreds of routes on the high peaks, the most well-known being the east face of Longs Peak, The Diamond. As well, there are thousands of other boulder problems scattered about the Front Range. Some of the best areas are Red Feather Lakes and the Poudre Canyon west of Ft. Collins, Eldorado Canyon, Boulder Canyon, The Flatirons, and the St. Vrain Canyon west of Boulder, and Clear Creek Canyon, Morrison, and the Matthews-Winters Park, west of Denver. There are several lifetimes of climbing in Colorado.

Visit Denver/Boulder: In addition to all of the great climbing, Denver and Boulder both make worthy visits on their own. Boulder has a reputation as the outdoor sports capital of the country. There are hundreds of miles of trails in the area for hiking, riding and running, as well as opportunities to fish, paddle, climb and sightsee. The Flatirons are a great place to start, as is Eldorado Canyon, just south of Boulder. The Shakespeare festival in the summer is just one of many great cultural events held here throughout the year. Denver is home to a wonderful art museum, an aquarium, and several professional sports teams. Red Rocks, just west of Denver, is one of the best musical venues in the country, and it attracts artists all summer.

Entry Passes to RMNP

To enter RMNP, you have to pay. There are a number of options for passes one can purchase.

Automobile Pass

Cost: $20. This pass is valid for 7 days.

RMNP Annual Pass

Cost: $40. This pass provides unlimited entry into RMNP for one year from the date of purchase. It also allows the holder to use the express lane (the far right lane of the Beaver Meadows Entrance), which can be very helpful on busy summer days. The time saved by using this lane is well worth the $40. This is the best option for almost everyone interested in visiting RMNP for more than a week.

America the Beautiful—National Parks and Recreational Lands Annual Pass

Cost: $80. This pass allows unlimited access into any National Park or National Fee Area—including the toll road to the summit of Mt. Evans. A good option if you plan on visiting other National Parks during the year, or if you plan on driving up the Mt. Evans Scenic Hwy. It does not grant the holder access to the express lane, which can lead to long waits at the gate. Occasionally, on very busy summer weekends, this pass will get you through the express lane if it's managed by a ranger, but this cannot be counted on.

Check out RMNP website for more information: www.nps.gov/romo/planyourvisit/feesandreservations.htm

Parking in RMNP, and the Shuttle Bus

The Park is a busy place during the summer. The main parking lots which access the boulders (Bear Lake Parking Lot and Glacier Gorge Parking Lot) are very popular and can fill up well before noon, especially on the weekends. To avoid the congestion, an option is to take the free shuttle offered by the Park.

The shuttle operates from the end of June until the beginning of September. Park and Ride (the place to park, leave your car, and get on the bus) is located just opposite the Glacier Basin Campground on the right side of the Bear Lake Road, 5.2 miles from the Beaver Meadows Entrance, and five miles from the turn-off onto Bear Lake Road. The buses run every 10–15 minutes, will make room for your crashpad, and stop at all the main trailheads which access the boulders. The last bus leaves Bear Lake at 7:30 pm promptly. If you've ridden the bus up, make sure to give yourself plenty of time to hike back down to the parking lot in time. If you miss the bus, you are looking at a 4.5-mile hike back down the road, which can be extremely unpleasant after a long day of bouldering.

The turquoise waters of Lake Haiyaha. Photo by Caroline Treadway

Rocky Mountain National Park Etiquette

Bouldering in the Park is a privilege and climbers should do everything they can to preserve and protect the resource and our opportunity to climb there. It is the responsibility of every visitor to know the rules and regulations that govern RMNP. Remember, you are in an area regulated by the federal government, and breaking the law is a federal offense.

Stashing gear, including crashpads, overnight is forbidden by Park rules. This is one issue the rangers have been very outspoken about and it is the number-one thing climbers can do to maintain the good relationship that exists between the Park and climbers. DON'T STASH YOUR PAD.

Pof should never be used. It can permanently change the texture of the rock, especially when mixed with chalk. Chalk (magnesium carbonate) is acceptable. Brush off your tick marks when you are finished at an area.

CHIPPING is absolutely not permitted, as it not only is destructive, it is in violation of Park rules as well. DO NOT CHIP HOLDS.

Clean up your trash. It takes a few seconds to double check an area before you leave, and if you drop a toothbrush or water bottle in among the rocks make a good effort and fish it out.

Cutting down trees or removal of vegetation is strictly forbidden by Park rules and regulations.

Do not harass, approach or feed the wildlife.

Stay on marked trails, or social trails described in the text, when possible. Avoid trampling vegetation. In Upper Chaos it is easy to always stay on rock.

Leave your music at home. While climbers can and do bring iPods with speakers to the boulders, this is often looked down upon, as it intrudes on other's ability to enjoy the silence. Remember, many visitors don't care about your techno music. Headphones make a great compromise. Be respectful of others' right to enjoy the area.

Tourists will most certainly ask about the crashpad on your back. Being courteous and taking the time to answer a few quick questions can go a long way toward establishing a positive image. Don't be rude.

Fires are strictly prohibited in Upper and Lower Chaos Canyon, Veritas, Stinkbug, Moraine Park and Emerald Lake.

There are no dogs allowed on trails in RMNP.

Shannon Forsman and Eric "EZ" Harrison hiking their pads out of Upper Chaos. Photo by Wade David

Dave Graham

An Interview by Jamie Emerson

On a beautiful spring day in 2011, Dave Graham and I hopped in his car and drove into an obscure canyon south of Estes Park on the hunt for new rock. Dave was intrumental in the development of RMNP and did the first ascents of many of the hardest problems there. We had a chance to talk about his involvement in this development, how he thinks it has changed over the years and what it meant for him to discover such an amazing place at the age of 18.

Jamie: What does Chaos Canyon mean to you?

Dave: Well, what shapes the opportunities for bouldering in Colorado? Why do things happen here when they happen? We talk about why the development of the Park was integral to American bouldering in a sense that it showed people that just because Chris Sharma didn't think it was impressive, that didn't mean it wouldn't be a haven for people who are interested in proving their climbing, and dedicating themselves to something they loved. Essentially what Chaos Canyon was, for a small group of people, it was a very inspiring thing. And that's all it took for that one group of people to come together, and for Chaos Canyon to be perceived as the hip, cool thing to do.

Now, ironically, the way things concrete themselves in climbing is that multiple generations appreciate something, right? We're still in the position where we just went to Castle Rocks and City of Rocks, in Idaho, where people have been climbing for 20 years and looking for boulders.

We're so far misplaced in our perception of what is new. It's just re-approaching the same things that we see over and over again. That's a crucial statement right there. It's really one of the big benchmarks of climbing, that's existential. The observation of something over the course of generations. Each different group of climbers, and each different school of climbers will approach things in a different way.

It's interesting, because I came out from Maine, and got together with some people from Colorado and observed something, and then defined that it was good. This became accepted, and people got to work, on their own levels. Me getting to work, being from New England and having experience only in developing because that's all there really was, other than traditional climbing. When we came to the Park I mean all Luke (Parady) and I did was put up new boulder problems, because there weren't any boulder problems there. We didn't know the grades, we didn't really care. At that point in our experience, when we were 18 years old, in the Park for the first time, we were like "Wow! We can find all kinds of new problems and put them up! Let's do it!"

Early on you visited the mecca of American bouldering, Hueco Tanks, in Texas. How did that first trip to Hueco formulate your opinion of the park?

I likened it to a Hueco of gneiss. A Rumney-style bouldering area. Like Rumney rock, but polished, and the size of a Hueco Mountain. Like a mountain up inside a canyon. Imagination-land. It was top notch!

At that time, being 18 and having been only to Hueco and New England, did you think it would become such an iconic area for American bouldering?

We didn't come from a place of trying to repeat things. There was nothing established so we thought let's put some things up. At first we thought "Is this cool?" "Do you think people will think this is cool?"

I grew up with ocean, wooded hills and snow. For me to come to Chaos Canyon for the first time, it was my first time at altitude, it was my first time in the Rocky Mountains, it was my first time in the West. It was AMAZING! It was this extremely beautiful, outrageously cool thing that I had never seen before. It was beyond cool. It was climbing at its best because it was this extreme destination with an extreme amount of rock.

In terms of the hiking, the poor landings, the altitude and the weather, it is striking, because no one had ever done anything like this before.

No one had ever been like "This is SICK," and I was like, "I am pretty sure this is SICK," and I don't think anybody is going to be able to tell me it's not. And that is when I fell in love with developing rock climbing because looking around Chaos Canyon I found more projects than I could do in a lifetime and I still probably won't do all the ones I found in the first season.

Most of the first year revolved around climbing in Lower Chaos. Did you hike into Upper Chaos that first season?

Yeah a little bit. I didn't find Jade that year, but I made it to that second level, and I was blown away. The next season, when I came back to develop Upper Chaos, I was trying to tell people at that point about the potential. I was immediately met with that same thing I've always been met with, which is people telling me that it is not that cool; that they don't want to go.

When I moved to Colorado, I moved here because of the Park. I went there in 2001 for the first time and I thought it was amazing. I think I probably saw what you saw, this incredible place in the mountains with sick boulders and I thought this was a perfect expression of rock climbing. The scenery is incredible...

You have to hike to it, it's located in a great place, it's aesthetic, its motivating, there are people here that are cool. These names are important: Herm Fiessner, Theo Merrin, Brian Capps, and Nick Sagar, led by Brian, because he was the one who I stayed with. Brian really introduced me to this place, and I must thank him. It is important to recognize that I would never have seen the Park without Brian Capps. I was so fortunate that he was so open with me as a young strong climber. Not being all competitive, but showing me things. So I was lucky that people were generous with me and shared things with me. Much like Lincoln Lake, how you (Jamie) were so open about that. And it saddens me now, in this day and age that people leave the work of developing new boulders to just a select few. That they won't even share the experience to go look at things, to take their time to go hike around. The real spirit behind the Park was shared among all these individuals to develop something amazing that existed, that was there, in nature, and to take full advantage of what we had been given. Not in a religous way, but if God's country existed, this is it, and we don't have to appreciate God to be in God's country. We were in one of the most beautiful places you could possibly be in, doing something special that was temporary, and we were all aware of what it would be someday because we weren't naive and oblivious to human culture and society. We knew how Boulder functioned. With the grades, we were very open. It could be this, it could be that. We don't know. We were very open about projects. We were very open about every single type of rock climb. We weren't criticising people's efforts. It was a very positive experience. And that, right there is something very archaic in the Boulder climbing scene. So there were all these thing that went into making it very special. And it was because of people's attitudes and their willingness to go out and do things together, that they wouldn't normally do.

You've been coming to the Park since 2000, and it's hard for me not to notice some of the changes we've both seen. Certainly in the physical nature of the area, but also in people's attitudes about what the Park means. Let's talk about some of the changes you've seen in the last 11 years.

One big change is, the ambitions of the people going there today don't seem so hinged on the comaraderie. It seems that their goals aren't to experience some form of comaraderie and to have an adventure with their friends. I feel like the goals have been much more influenced by the gym climbing scene. There was an age where it started to become more important to go up to the Park to send and if you weren't going up to the Park to send then you weren't doing anything. I feel like it was really important to recognize the era when you just went up and tried projects and you just worked on things. It wasn't very productive, but at the same time there wasn't anybody judging you. There was a shift when the climbing scene in Boulder become so full of climbers that there started to be this Neighborhood Watch; like who's doing what and when and how. It seemed much more critical than constructive. In the beginning, I feel like the things that were the most important to the climbers changed. The values that they judged their day on changed. It was more like, "Did you send two 8Bs today?" It seemed like if you didn't send two 8B's then you had a reason to be bummed. Back in the day there was never a reason to be bummed walking out of the Park because it was such a beautiful place, we were just like, "Wow, this is such a gorgeous place" and there was nowhere to report it anyway, and nobody even really wrote an article about it. We didn't get press on the Park because it wasn't cool, and it seemed to go unnoticed. Same with Ticino, in Switzerland.

How do you feel visiting the Park now?

I get very frustrated that no one is interested in looking for new boulders. People just want to repeat stuff. I just want to try all of the new projects and everyone is just like, "I just want to repeat this thing man" and then I get kinda bummed. There are so many amazing things to go do and it is so motivating. If I go with the right people then it's just like the old days!

History

Rocky Mountain National Park has a long and rich history of climbing. Its steep faces, solid rock and dramatic setting have made it one of the premier alpine rock destinations in America. Only recently have climbers turned their attention to the massive talus fields and glacial erratics that litter the forest floor.

John Gill was one of the first climbers to boulder in the region. He put up problems at the now closed Hagermeister Boulders in Estes Park. It would be years before climbers started looking to the base of the high peaks, and development was slow. Many of the landings in the Park are jumbled, and the severely overhanging nature of the climbs nearly requires a posse with crashpads.

Climbers had been climbing on the boulders at the base of Lumpy Ridge for years, but it wasn't until the 1990s those standards were pushed up into the V10 range with problems like Livid Man (aka Right Angry Man) V10 and Sap V9. Climbers like Dean Potter, Jim Belcer, Jim Hurst, Pete Zoller, Matt Samet and Ian Glas were all frequenting Lumpy Ridge and, soon after, Emerald Lake. The introduction of the commercial crashpad opened up new possibilities for steeper and harder climbing.

The first place boulderers pushed into the mountains was Emerald Lake. In 1990 or '91, Jim Hurst, who had been climbing Hallett Peak, noticed the amazing potential at Emerald Lake. He would go up with John Wallinford, but had trouble convincing other climbers that the two-mile hike was worth it. Hurst would guide Wallingford up the walls, if Wallingford would spot him on his projects. Jim put up the classic V5 "In Your Face" (which is now known as the The Kind) for a large block that threatened to (and evenutally did) come off. Hurst went so far as to ski up early in the year, and climb on problems whose landings were filled in with snow, fixing the crashpads in place with ski poles. Hurst eventually convinced Dean Potter, Jim Belcer, Steph Davis, Bronson McDonald and Ian Glas to join him. The Park was perhaps the first alpine area of its kind in America, and this group laid the foundation for that development. Ian Glas did the first ascent of The Kind Traverse V11 at Emerald Lake a few years later. At the time this was one of the hardest problems in the state. More importantly, it opened the door for hard bouldering high in the mountains. Many of the hardest problems in Colorado today are found in the Park, and The Kind Traverse was the first. Development again slowed, however, as this new approach was not quick to gain acceptance. It wasn't until 1998 when local Mike Caldwell, father of all-around great Tommy Caldwell, made his way to Lake Haiyaha looking for a good trout-fishing spot. He returned to tell Tommy about the hundreds of boulders surrounding the lake, and that fall, Tommy, Herman Fiessner, Theo Merrin, Brian Capps and Nick Sagar made their way up to the boulders. The first few days Tommy climbed the classic Tommy's Arête V7 and Potato Chip V7. Brian did the first ascent of Handicapps V9, although this was originally graded V8, and Nick put up the Skyscraper V5 and The Marble V10 (at the time).

The next year proved to be pivotal. Dave Graham was a young climber from Maine who displayed tremendous raw talent from the beginning. He had been traveling out west, working his way through some of the hardest sport routes in Rifle, and was still quite an up and comer. He and Brian Capps had met in Rifle and Brian took Dave to Chaos Canyon to check out some new bouldering. Brian says that Dave didn't do too much in the first few days but after warming up to the elevation, the hike, and the bad landings, he began to leave a permanent mark on some of the best stone in the West.

That year (2000) Dave established most of the problems in Lower Chaos. On one of his more impressive days he climbed the first ascent of Freshly Squeezed and Bushpilot, calling the former V10 or V11 and the latter V9. He also did the FA of The Automator V13, The Centaur V12, The Gobot V11, The Fat Lady V10, Deep Puddle Dynamics V9 and Gang Bang Arête V8. This frenzy culminated in Nuthin' but Sunshine, which Dave graded V14, even though he had never repeated a problem V13 or harder. At the time Dave was 19. There were a handful of problems that were V12 or harder in the US, and almost all of them were in Hueco Tanks, TX. His vision for hard climbing, at such a young age, is astounding. Some of these problems have since been downgraded, but it is clear now that Dave was well ahead of the curve. The internet was not the force it is today and information was slow to spread.

The old website www.newenglandbouldering.com had some enthusiastic reports of the initial development:

9/13/00 Rocky Mountain National Park, CO: Dave Graham has spent most of the summer out west, and most of his time putting up new boulder

Theo Merrin attempts European Human Being circa 2000. Photo by Brian Capps

problems in Rocky Mountain National Park. Dave says about this area, "This place is FIVE STAR!!!! as high quality as Hueco, stone as bullet as Rumney, and a location uncomparable to any other bouldering that isn't at 12,000 feet! AMAZING. I must emphasize the quality of stone, aesthetics, and good lines. I have never bouldered anywhere like it." Dave said that the area had not really been developed and felt lucky to stumble upon so many hard projects. Here is list of some of the highlights:—The Automator, maybe hard V12, maybe harder, took three or four days—The Centaur, V12 maybe harder, took five days this past spring—European human being, V12, hard 5 move power problem. Luke Parady and Dave did this problem over three days, and they both think it's harder than Diaphanous Sea at Hueco—Fat Lady, V10+, repeated by Nick Sagar and Theo Merrin—The Gobot, V10+, unrepeated, 25 feet of power endurance climbing, Ghetto Simulator-like landing—Optimus Prime, V9/10?, BAD landing, like a ten foot pit—Deep Puddle Dynamics, V9, high and proud, 100% slopers-very atypical of the Park, you top out three times!—Gang Bang Arête, V8, easiest of the moderates—but hard V8—classic. Dave said there are about three other really hard projects he wants to do. One, he worked on four days this past spring, and one day so far this fall. Dave says, "It is amazing, the best line, the best holds—rad hard, maybe V14." Stay tuned for the news on the send.

The next year was more of the same as Dave and his good buddy Chad Greedy marched up the hill and put up classics like Left El Jorge V11, Eternia V11 (although Dave originally suggested V13), Skipper Roof, Golden Rows of Flows and countless other problems that may go unrecorded. Dave seemed unstoppable and climbed nearly every line he put chalk on. His efforts put Rocky Mountain National Park on the map and even today, 10 years later, people line up to repeat these great boulders.

Around this same time Paul Otis, Jon Linhart, Jim Belcer, Tom Moulin and others picked some of the easier plums, and began to hike farther up the canyon. Paul climbed the FA of Full Chaos V10, an outstanding problem almost three miles from the car, and a full 30 min past Eternia, and Belcer climbed Mr. Hanky V9.

Dave returned in 2003 from Switzerland to hike even farther up Tyndall Gorge in the Park. There, above Emerald Lake at the Hallett Boulder, he established several hard problems including Fireball V10 and Stranger in a Strange Land V12. James Litz also climbed in the Park that year, and besides climbing nearly every hard problem in a matter of a couple weeks, in less than ideal conditions, he added the hardest problem to date, Freaks of the Industry V13.

Daniel Woods was coming of age in the following years and he set his sights on repeating all of the classics and putting up some of his own. Daniel worked his way through Freaks of the Industry, Nuthin' But Sunshine, Freshly Squeezed. Daniel could run laps on The Automator and at one point climbed Tommy's Arête blindfolded. Clearly he was ready for a greater challenge. In 2001, Dave had found a massive boulder in Chaos Canyon and on its north face lies an impressive overhang. It was known for years as "The Green 45" and it held the one thing that shut Dave down. He was the only one to

Wade David on the hunt for new problems. Photo by Jason Pinto

do "the move" but no one else was even close. Fast forward to 2007. Daniel Woods, honed on all of Dave's hardest problems, made the first ascent of Jade V15, the hardest problem in Colorado.

In a somewhat unexpected twist, the next few years of development focused not on hiking further upcanyon, but filling in the gaps, with surprisingly excellent results. Further development continued with problems like Top Notch V13, Tyler Landman's classic addition that climbers had walked by for years, and a contender for one of the hardest moves in the Park. The gaps continued to be filled in this same manner, as a wide range of climbers added singular problems. Nic Sherman climbed Wildcat V12, Andre DiFelice sent the gorgeous overhang Pterodactyl V12, Phil Schaal climbed the classic I Comb My Hair Like God V11 and Paul Robinson put up the spectacular roof Riddles in the Park V12. Paul and Ty would go on to repeat Jade, and the frenzy of bouldering in the alpine zones in the summer reached a peak. In a matter of a few years, alpine bouldering went from being virtually unknown, to being the testing grounds for the strongest climbers in the world.

Dave Graham makes the FA of The Green Arête, as Chad Greedy provide a good spot. Photo by Jorge Visser

More new faces arrived, either permanently or on vacation. Phil Schaal, Jimmy Webb and Carlo Traversi all made repeats of Jade and downgraded it to V14, possibly after the crux hold became better (although the improvement was minimal, and few think it was actually chipped). Regardless, the Park was firmly established as one of the best places to boulder in the world.

In 2008 Angela Payne made an impressive ascent of European Human Being V12, in Lower Chaos. At the time this was the hardest problem climbed in the US by a female and Payne spent three years, finally hiking up by herself, setting a camera on a rock to record her ascent, and climbing the short testpiece. Alex Puccio followed with ascents of The Marble Sit V11 and The Centaur V12, but in the summer of 2010 Payne climbed The Automator V13. This was the first established V13 climbed by a woman, anywhere in the world. This ascent continued in the tradition of standard-setting climbing high in the mountains of Colorado.

Adam Strong, Melissa Strong, Kevin Cuckovich, Glenn and Heather Johnson, Bronson McDonald and Matt Tschol have all been dedicated locals summering in Estes Park for a number of years.

As the lower sections of Chaos Canyon became fully developed, climbers began looking higher. In the summer of 2010 Jon Glassberg and Ryan Silven began to climb where others had only looked, and added some excellent new boulders, in a move that acknowledges the future. There are still hundreds of unclimbed boulders in this magnificent canyon, and the intrepid boulderer will find a lifetime of climbing in the upper reaches of this amazing place.

n Glassberg bears down on the terrible sloper of Both Sides of the Spectrum V12. Photo by Jon Glassberg Collection

Moraine Park

The bouldering in Moraine Park provides a nice contrast to Chaos Canyon and Emerald Lake. Set in a low-lying forest, along a beautiful stream, this is a small but worthwhile area. It is not uncommon to spot elk or moose near the Big Thompson River, which flows peacefully through the valley. Arch Rocks is the specific name given on Park maps to the area, although most climbers refer to the climbing here as Moraine Park. The elevation of the bouldering in Moraine Park is 8,235 ft.

Season

Moraine Park and Arch Rocks are at a much lower elevation than most of the bouldering in RMNP. While it stays cool in the forest during the summer, this area is best to visit in October and November, when the high alpine areas are snowy and the aspen are golden. It is also the first area to melt out in the spring, and the motivated can climb here as early as March and April. The summer can be reasonable in the evening, but it can also be greasy on the bullet-hard granite. This area is a good alternative if rained or snowed out of Chaos Canyon or Emerald Lake.

Approach

From the park entrance at Highway 36, drive 0.2 miles and turn left onto Bear Lake Road. Drive 1.3 miles and turn right onto Moraine Park Road. Follow this for 0.6 miles to the Moraine Park Campground. Turn left (the road to the campground is straight) for 1.3 miles to the Cub Lake Trailhead. Continue past a parking lot for 0.9 miles to the terminus of the road and the Fern Lake Trailhead (elev. 8,165 ft). Park here. There is additional parking back down along the road. In the winter, the last 0.9 miles must be hiked, as the one-lane dirt road is gated shut.

Hike the Fern Lake Trail for one mostly flat mile to Arch Rocks. The approach takes about 25 minutes. There are a number of scattered boulders along the trail and up the hill on the right. Several projects await, and this is somewhat of an exploratory area. The best, established problems are listed here.

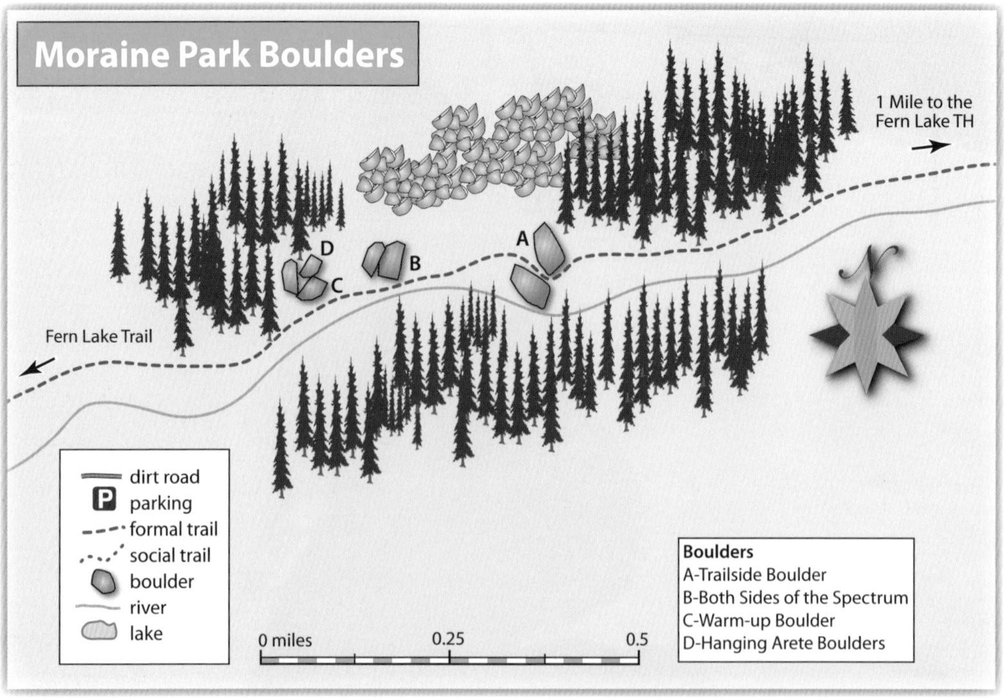

Looking across Moraine Park towards Arch Rocks

A. Trailside Boulder

Approximately one mile from the Fern Lake Trailhead, this massive boulder will come into view, just a few yards from the trail. The trail winds around the left side of the boulder. These problems are very near, or even on the trail. Please be courteous to hikers.

❒ 1. **Lip Traverse V7** ★★
Start on the far left side of the lip, traverse to the arête and topout.

❒ 2. **Dave's Problem V9** ★★★
This problem is around the left side of the boulder. Start standing, on a small left-hand sidepull and a right-hand sloping edge. Climb straight up the face.
FA David Graham 2003

❒ 3. **The Werewolf V10**
Continue upcanyon on the main trail and around the left side of the boulder. Start standing on a right-hand thin edge and a high left-hand sloper. Climb straight up to a flat jug and drop off. The good sloping hold out left, just up from the starting hold, is off.
FA Tommy Caldwell 2003

Trailside Boulder

Trailside Boulder

Trailside Boulder

Bouldering in RMNP

Tommy Caldwell

It was my dad who first mentioned it, "Have you ever seen the boulders around Lake Haiyaha? You should hike up there and take a look." Now, 11 years later, I can't believe climbers had missed a truly world-class bouldering area for so long. I guess it's no mystery that the discovery of the high peaks bouldering in Colorado coincides with the invention of big foam bouldering pads. Take away the pads and the boulders look a lot less appealing. But still, now that I know what to look for, I can see the boulderfield from my house 20 miles away.

The first time I walked up to Chaos Canyon I nearly blew a fuse. I ran around, peeking in all the holes, adrenaline pumping. It was like I was on crack…way too good to be true and totally overwhelming. To me it was like finding lost treasure. I explored for days; all the way up to the glacier. I then came back with a few friends. Our first day climbing, a small group of us established some of the classics like Potato Chip, Tommy's Arête and Autobot, although at that time there were too many to name. The rock was perfect and took no cleaning! After word got out the place exploded like a firecracker. I left on an expedition for two months and when I returned there were 20 people at the boulders. That summer Dave Graham climbed some of the modern test pieces like Nothin' But Sunshine and The Automator. Colorado bouldering has never been the same.

I grew to love the thin mountain air, intense thunderstorms and the light twinkling off the lake. For a while it was my place to escape and find peace, but also my place to get strong. In recent years it has become my summertime climbing gym. The powerful nature of the climbing in Chaos Canyon is the best training I have found, and it's no secret. People are flocking from all over the world to test themselves on some of the hardest boulder problems in the world on these high-altitude blocks.

B. Both Sides of the Spectrum

Continue on the trail 20 yds upcanyon from The Werewolf. All of the problems are on the right side of the trail.

❒ 1. **Both Sides of the Spectrum V12** ★★★★
Start standing, matched on a flat edge. Make a huge move to a terrible sloper out left. This beautiful problem is one of the most coveted ticks in the Park. The quality of the rock, uniqueness of movement and beautiful setting make it an unrivaled classic. The longstanding "Karma Project."
FA Harry Robertson 2007

❒ 2. **V5** ★★
Start sitting on a flat jug, climb up and left to the arête. Hard. Great rock.

C. Warm Up Boulder

Right off the trail, 10 yds beyond Both Sides of the Spectrum. Good rock and friendly holds make this the best place to warm up. Several variations exist.

❒ 1. **V5** ★★
Start sitting on a low edge. Move to two crimps and dyno to the lip. The dyno itself is V4.

❒ 2. **V4** ★★
Start sitting on a flat jug and climb up.

D. Hanging Arête Boulders

Just behind the Warm Up Boulder.

❒ 1. **Undercling Roof V8** ★★
Start standing, matched on a flat undercling in the roof.

❒ 2. **Hanging Arête V6** ★★★
Start standing on a right-hand sloping ball, and a left hand on a very thin crimp. Climb the compression feature.

iel Woods makes the first ascent of the hardest problem in Colorado, Hypnotized Minds V15. Photo by Steve Woods

Veritas Boulder

Veritas is a massive glacial erratic that lies just off the road. The elevation is 8,927 ft.

Season

The Veritas Boulder is typically climbable from mid-March through November, with the best conditions in early spring or late fall. It is most likely too hot in the middle of the summer, but the evenings can be cool. The Bear Lake Road is open year round, so this boulder can always be accessed. In the winter it is usually covered with snow. It stays mostly shaded.

Approach

From the park entrance on Highway 36 drive 0.2 miles. Turn left onto Bear Lake Road. Drive 7.2 miles, and park in a small gravel pullout on the left. Additional parking is 0.5 miles back down the road at the Bierstadt Lake Trailhead on the right, or 0.2 miles farther back down the road (from Bierstadt Lake Trailhead) at the Storm Pass Trailhead, on the left. If you park here, take care when hiking along the road. The shuttle bus also stops at Bierstadt Lake Trailhead and it's an easy 0.5 mile walk down the road, for those so inclined. The massive gray boulder, which lies buried in the hillside, is on the left side of the road. Hike downhill around the left side of the boulder.

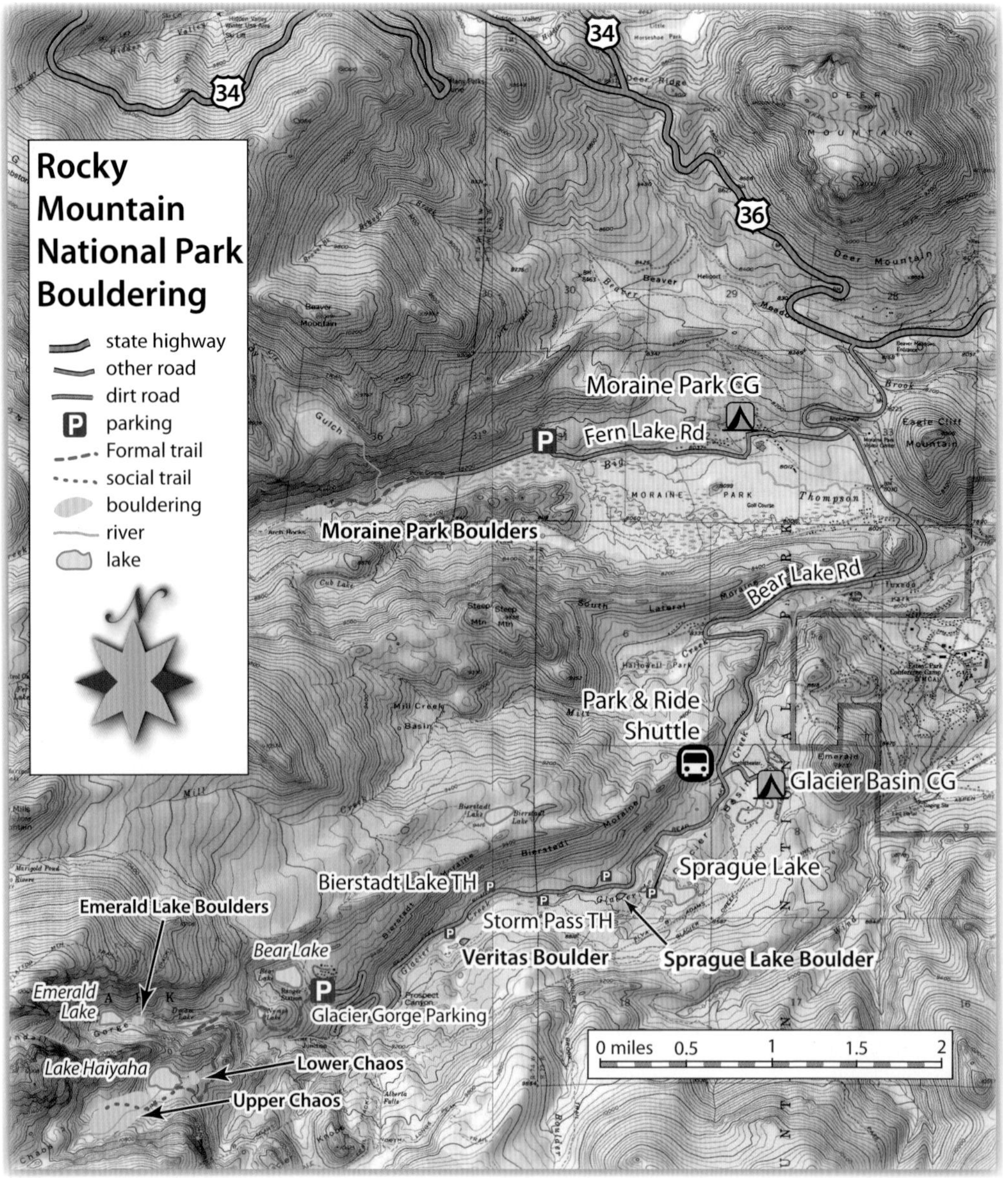

Veritas Boulder

❒ 1. **Stripes V9**
Stand start on a high right-hand edge, and a poor left-hand sidepull. Make a hard move to a good, left-hand edge.
FA Harry Robertson 2007

❒ 2. **Hypnotized Minds V15** ★★★
Start on Veritas Sit and climb right into the black face on very small crimps and an awful left-hand pinch.
FA Daniel Woods 2010

❒ 3. **Veritas V8** ★★
Stand start on a high undercling for the left hand and flat hold for the right hand. Climb straight up. Committing. In Roman mythology, Veritas is the goddess of truth.
FA Ken Kenny 2003

❒ 4. **Veritas Sit V11** ★★★★
This was a sit-start until a hold broke. Start squatting with a good right-hand gaston, where the angle of the offset changes slightly, and a lower left hand. Most climbers start with a high left foot on the big flake. A couple of moves lead to a very hard shoulder press to an undercling. The roadside approach, direct nature of the line, and amazing rock make this one of the most coveted ticks in the Park. An amazing problem.
FA Johnny Goicoechea 2006

❒ 5. **Mandix V10** ★
Start on Veritas and traverse the wall to the left, topping out up the arête.
FA Brian Camp 2009

❒ 6. **Veritas Low Left V12** ★★★
Start matched on a large flake to the left of Veritas Sit and climb right into Veritas.
FA David Graham 2008

❒ 7. **Mendax V13**
Start matched on a large flake, move up to a sloping, left-hand edge, then right hand to a terrible pinch. Move all the way to the lip. The arête was not used on the FA. Very contrived, and many variations exist.
FA Paul Robinson 2008

❒ 8. **Menwax V7**
Start matched on a large flake and climb left to the arête and up. The uncontrived version of Mendax.
FA Jamie Emerson 2008

❒ 9. **Bulgin' Out V8**
Around the left side of the boulder from Veritas. Start matched on a chest-high crimp. Climb straight up on pinches to a good jug.
FA Tyler Landman 2007

Daniel Woods

Daniel Woods, one of the most powerful climbers in the world. Photo by Daniel Woods Collection

I first heard of RMNP back in 2000, when Dave Graham established some of Colorado's hardest blocs at the time. Classics like Nuthin' But Sunshine, The Centaur, and Left El Jorge set the pace for what was about to go down in the years to come. The thing that makes RMNP so unique for me is the high alpine adventure feel. It takes about 45 minutes to hike up to Lower Chaos Canyon aka Lake Haiyaha, and another 30 to reach Upper Chaos from there. Surrounding you is the Diamond of Longs Peak, Halletts Peak, and thin air.

The style is predominately fingery which means the holds are small incuts or flat edges. The climbing is very controlled with more static than dynamic movement. The Park really built up my finger strength and taught me how to move precisely with my feet and hands. After Dave left his mark, Paul Robinson, Ty Landman, and myself set out to explore both canyons for more potential. Over the course of a couple years, problems like Secret Splendour, Element of Suprise, Top Notch, Don't Get Too Greedy, Blood Money, and Aslan arose.

My goal was to find a project that sort of stood out from all the rest, and this came when I heard about the Green 45 project. This was a green, lichen filled wall which towered 25 feet at a 45 degree angle. The lower half involved intense crimping leading to a victory ledge, where you could casually stroll to the top. The theme of the problem revolved around "the Move." This involved taking a one-finger divot for the middle finger and subtly sliding in the ring and index finger onto the sloping outskirts, compressing the ring finger, which triggered my brain that I was actually holding onto something. After taking this hold, you made an iron cross move out left to a quarter-pad credit-card-slot edge. The outro moves clocked in at 7C+ to the jug. This was by far the hardest thing I had tried at the time and motivation to do it was high.

On a crisp June night (around midnight), I fired the first ascent, naming the line Jade, and proposing 8C. I had repeated multiple established 8B+ problems at the time, so it seemed logical to say this was harder than all the rest. It is a very specialized climb and involves freezing conditions and perfect skin. After many repeats over the years, Jade has settled at 8B+. I have recently gone up and repeated it confirming the downgrade, but the important thing to me was that this climb made me realize the beauty of trying an inspiring piece of rock, working moves, and eventually sending the impossible. I have taken what I experienced with Jade to other areas in Colorado and around the world to continue pushing my climbing limits. Just recently, I established another line on the Veritas boulder, which I named Hypnotized Minds. I am proposing 8C and feel like it is the second-hardest climb (next to The Game) I have ever done.

There are so many strong and motivated climbers in Colorado, and having this kind of scene allows for many new problems and areas to be established. Nowadays, I use RMNP as a day of exploration, training, or rest. It makes me feel like I am at home and healthy. I am excited for the years to come at the Park.

Jamie Emerson sticks the first move of Lonestar V10. Photo by Sockhands Collection

Stinkbug Boulder

From the park entrance on Highway 36 drive 0.2 miles and turn left onto Bear Lake Road. Take Bear Lake Road for 8.5 miles to the Glacier Gorge Trailhead (elevation 9,240 ft) on the left. Park here. This small parking lot is often full, as the Glacier Gorge Trailhead accesses some of the most spectacular hiking in the Park. It's best to arrive early in the morning or late in the evening. The shuttle bus can be a good option during the busy season. Continuing on the established trail to Alberta Falls for 0.4 mile is a worthwhile side trip. Stinkbug itself sits at an elevation of 9,547 ft, 307 feet above the trailhead.

Season

Climbable typically from about mid-March through November. Most likely too hot in the middle of the summer, but evenings can be cool. Conditions are best in the spring and fall. Generally this area stays cooler than Veritas, but warmer and much less snowy than Emerald Lake or Chaos Canyon.

Approach

From the Glacier Gorge Trailhead, hike 0.25 miles crossing a sturdy bridge halfway. Turn left on the Loch Vale and Alberta Falls Trail. Take this for 150 yds through a grove of aspen to a small bridge. Just before the bridge, head diagonally right into the woods, following a faint social trail. Pick your way through the trees for about 50 yds, heading for the left side of a 200 ft cliff. Head around the left side of the cliff. Hike steeply up the hillside. There is no trail here, but make your way west and up towards the top of the ridge. Gain the top of the ridge and hike for another 100 yds or so, west (away from the cliff) to a small saddle. The Stinkbug Boulder is here, facing north. A very nice piece of overhanging rock and often a place of solitude. Spectacular vistas abound.

If the Glacier Gorge Trailhead is full, there is another way to access Stinkbug, and although it is longer, it is still a good option. Continue past the Glacier Gorge Parking area on Bear Lake Road until it deadends at the Bear Lake Parking lot. This is a large parking area with one trailhead at the end of the lot. Pass the Ranger Station that marks the trailhead (elev. 9,450 ft) on the left and cross a footbridge into the forest. Turn left, and then take the left fork, to Glacier Gorge, for 0.5 miles. At the trail junction, continue straight towards Alberta Falls. Take this for 150 yds through a grove of aspen and a small bridge. Follow the instructions above.

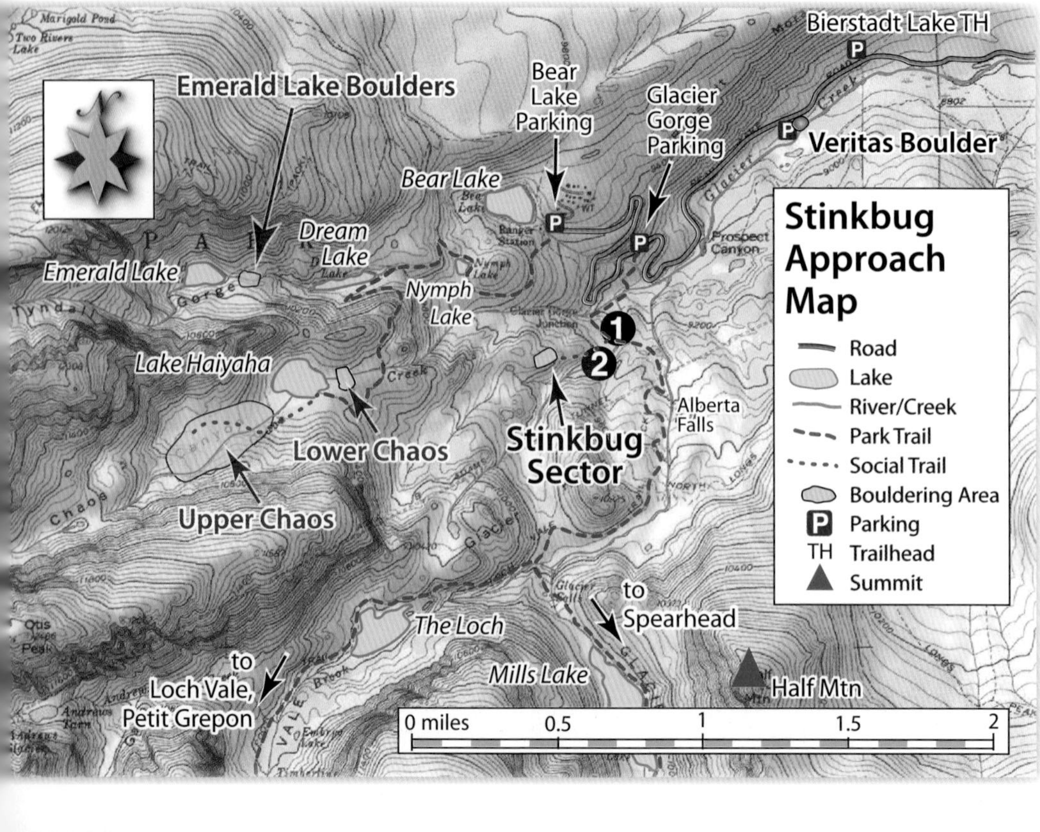

Stinkbug Approach

Stinkbug Approach

Glacier Creek flows swiftly in spring, near Stinkbug. Photo: Caroline Treadway

Stinkbug Boulder

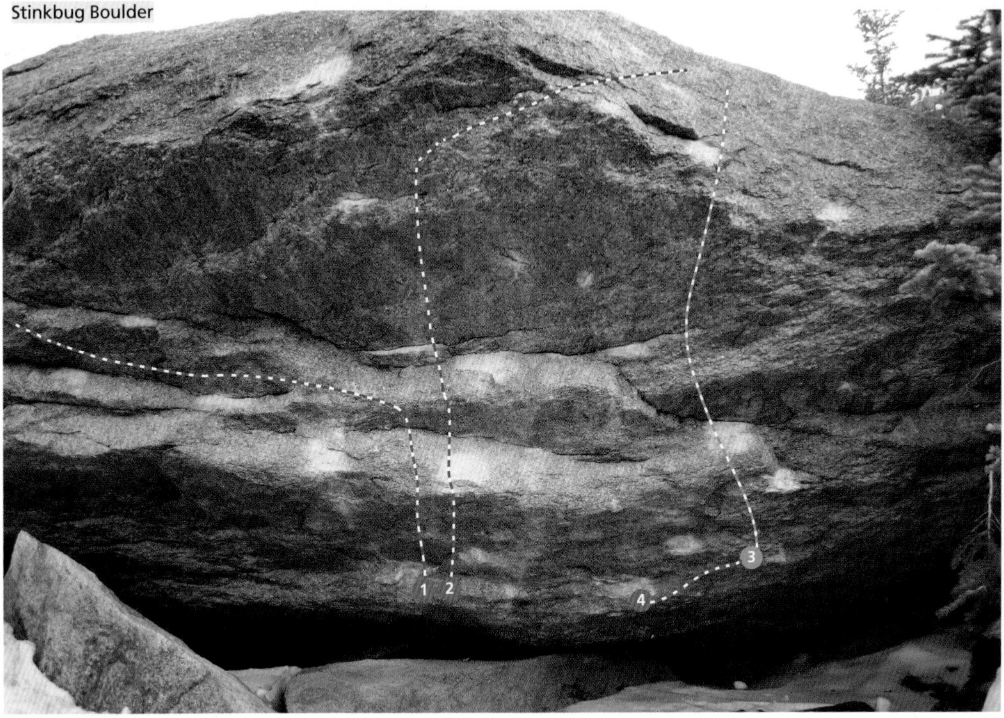

A. Stinkbug Boulder

❒ 1. **Stinkbug Variation V10** ★
Start sitting on a left-hand crimp and a small right-hand pinch. Make a huge move to a sloper, but head left after the first three moves.
FA Brian Camp 2008

❒ 2. **Lonestar aka Stinkbug V10** ★★★
Start sitting on a left-hand crimp and a small right-hand pinch. Make a huge move to a sloper, and finish straight up the overhang, topping out slightly right. Tommy Caldwell's original name was Lonestar, but Hank Jones renamed it Stinkbug, for the way the climber clamped on with their feet for the opening moves. Most refer to it now as Stinkbug. Classic, and unique.
FA Tommy Caldwell 2003

❒ 3. **Finite Endeavors V9** ★★
Start sitting on two opposing sidepull crimps. Climb straight up, right of Stinkbug.
"We can find infinite pleasure in our finite endeavors"
-Friedrich Nietzsche
FA Jamie Emerson 2004

❒ 4. **The Power of Ten V12** ★★
Start matched on a crescent-shaped crimp. Climb into the start of #3, and finish on that.
FA Tyler Landman 2007

There are several other variations (that have been omitted from the photo for clarity) which exist and they are as follows:

❒ 5. **Infinite Stink V10** ★★
Start on #3 and after the first three moves, head left and finish on #2.
FA Justin Jaeger 2008

❒ 6. **Lone Endeavors V10** ★★
Start on #1 and after the first four moves, head right and finish on #3.
FA Jamie Emerson 2008

RMNP4 Emerald Lake

Japanese climbers Aya Onoe (climbing), Tomoko Ogawa (center) and Humiki Asada (right) enjoying the classic bouldering at Emerald Lake. Photo by Susanica Tam

Emerald Lake

The bouldering at Emerald Lake is spectacular, with massive boulders standing stoically underneath the looming east face of Hallett Peak, among waterfalls and wildflowers. The 1.5 mile hike gains 605 ft. The elevation is 10,080 ft.

Season

The season here begins around the beginning of May, but expect hiking over packed snow and, potentially, bitter wind, snow and cold that early in the year. This area dries out quickly and is climbable into late October.

Approach

From the park entrance on Highway 36 drive 0.2 miles and turn left onto Bear Lake Road. Take Bear Lake Road for 10.0 miles to the Bear Lake Parking Lot at the end of the road. Park here. It's best to arrive early in the morning or after 3pm, especially on the weekends. The Bear Lake Parking Lot is a large parking area with one trailhead at its western end. From the Bear Lake Parking Lot and the Bear Lake Trailhead, pass the ranger station on your left and cross a footbridge into the forest. Turn left, passing the Glacier Gorge Junction Trail on your left. The Emerald Lake Trail (a paved path) leads uphill into the forest. The pavement disappears shortly before Nymph Lake (elev. 9,700 ft), which appears through the trees at 0.6 miles, on the left. Continue around the lake and uphill several hundred yards, to expansive views of Glacier Gorge and Longs Peak. Continue on the trail uphill, crossing Tyndall Creek on a footbridge. In 70 yds is a trail junction. Take the right fork to Emerald Lake. From the junction, continue along the shore of Dream Lake (elev. 9,900 ft) on the Emerald Lake Trail. At the far end of the lake the trail heads uphill through the trees, emerging from the woods below a large cliffband on the left. Continue to a small footbridge. Just past the footbridge, step through a small cluster of trees and head left, off the Emerald Lake Trail, over some logs. Move up and right over some rock slabs to the tall monolithic boulder, and after crossing small, bridgeless Tyndall Creek, head slightly left for 10 yds.

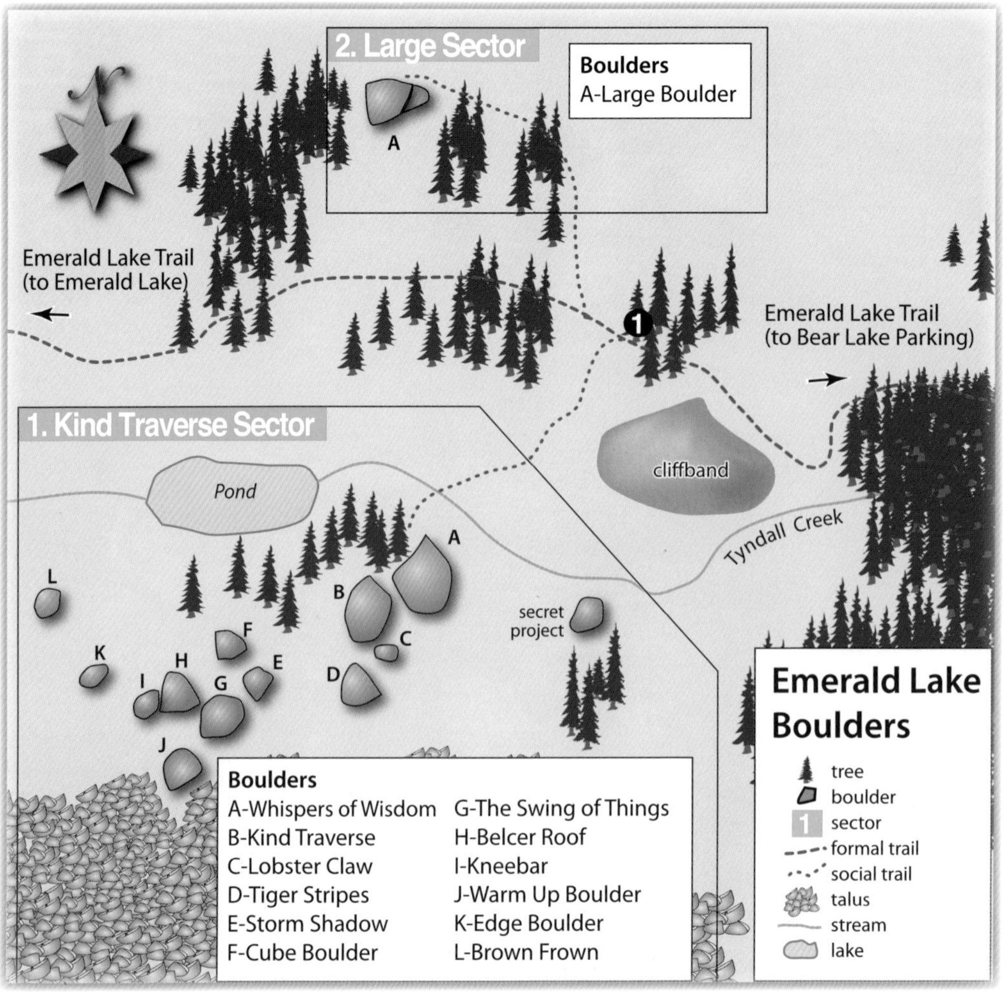

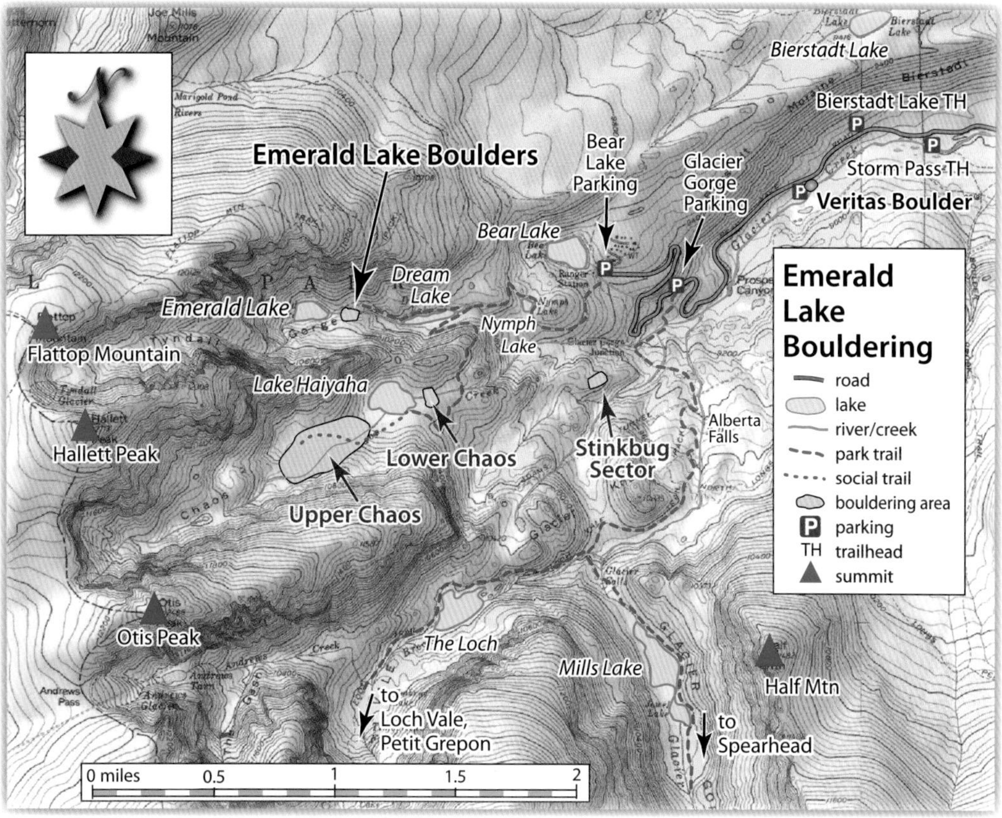
Emerald Lake Boulders
Bierstadt Lake
Bierstadt Lake TH
Bear Lake Parking
Glacier Gorge Parking
Storm Pass TH
Veritas Boulder
Bear Lake
Dream Lake
Emerald Lake
Nymph Lake
Flattop Mountain
Lake Haiyaha
Hallett Peak
Lower Chaos
Stinkbug Sector
Alberta Falls
Upper Chaos
Otis Peak
The Loch
Mills Lake
Half Mtn
to Loch Vale, Petit Grepon
to Spearhead
0 miles 0.5 1 1.5 2
Emerald Lake Bouldering
road
lake
river/creek
park trail
social trail
bouldering area
parking
TH trailhead
summit

Whispers of Wisdom
social trail to the Kind Traverse Sector
Emerald Lake Trail
Getting There 1

Kind Traverse Sector

A. Whispers of Wisdom Boulder

After crossing Tyndall Creek, Whispers of Wisdom is slightly uphill on the left. This beautiful and majestic boulder is set beneath the towering walls and spires of Hallett Peak and Flattop Mountain.

❒ 1. **Whispers of Wisdom V10** ★★★★
Start squatting on a right-hand mini-pinch and a left-hand pinch/sidepull. Amazing compression climbing on near-perfect rock. Topout up the huge, but easy slab. Incredible views await the committed boulderer. This is one of the best problems in the country.
Adam Osterhoff is often credited with the FA, although Eric Decaria, in typically quiet fashion, claims the actual first ascent a year or two before Adam. The benchmark for V10 in RMNP.

❒ 2. **Whispers Arête V7** ★
Start sitting with a left-hand sidepull and a right hand on a flat edge on the right side of the arête. Head up and finish the same as #1.
FA Eric Decaria circa 2002

❒ 3. **The Crack V7** ★
Start standing with a right-hand gaston and a left-hand sidepull. Climb up the crack and head right, underclinging out the roof to a hard encounter at the lip. The bold will topout up the dihedral. This can also be topped out at V7 straight up from the crack, on flat edges to an even scarier finish.

❒ 4. **Downclimb V0** ★
The easiest way to get on top of this monolithic boulder, this also serves as the downclimb.

Whispers of Wisdom is one of the most iconic hard problems in Colorado. The first ascent history is unclear. Adam Osterhoff is often credited for the FA, but in typically quiet fashion Eric Decaria suggests that he climbed the line a year or two before. Both climbers had to push their way through a dense pine tree that leaned against the left side of the lip for years until a snowstorm knocked it over, opening up this classic for everyone. The 35-ft slab that guards the summit is relatively easy, and remains a rite of passage for anyone wishing to claim an ascent. Photo by Sockhands Collection

The Kind Traverse Boulder

B. The Kind Traverse Boulder

This large boulder is just 10 yds upcanyon from Whispers of Wisdom.

❒ 1. **Warm Up V1** ★★

Sit start on low flat edges.

❒ 2. **Dave's Problem V12**

A contrivance, but listed for historical purposes. Start sitting on flat edges, move to a right-hand gaston, and then to a very small left-hand crimp. Finish on #3. Dave climbed this line after another climber challenged him to move off of the terribly small left-hand crimp.
FA David Graham 2001

❒ 3. **In Your Face aka The Kind V5** ★★★★

Start standing on a left-facing, sidepull jug, and climb up and right, on positive flat edges. One of the best problems in Colorado for the V5 grade. Outstanding. V6 from a sitdown start. Jim Hurst named the line "In Your Face" for a dangerous block that has since broken off, but it has become known recently as The Kind.
FA Jim Hurst '91 or '92

❒ 4. **Mr. Whimpy V7** ★

Start on In Your Face, head up and left, then back right. Contrived. V8 from a sitdown start.

❒ 5. **The Kind Traverse V11** ★★

Start standing on a left-facing, sidepull jug, and head left on polished rock. Great moves. This was flashed by Dave Graham in 2000. Low in the grade. Cicada Jenerik went low and left at the low flat edge, close to the ground. This bypasses the crux of the Kind Traverse, but remains an option for a shorter climber.
FA Ian Glass circa 1995

❒ 6. **The Full Kind Traverse V11** ★

Traverses the boulder, starting on #1 and finishing on #5. Go either high or low to get to the start of The Kind Traverse. Adds a V6 into #5. High in the grade.

C. Lobster Claw Boulder

Facing The Kind Traverse Boulder, walk left around the side of the boulder and up a small hill for 5 yds.

❒ 1. **Lobster Claw V4** ★

Start low in a small pit with crimps on the obvious sloping rail. Tension your way straight up with positive but small holds.

Lobster Claw

D. Tiger Stripes Boulder

Walk left around Lobster Claw and around a few smaller blocks for 30 yds to some trees, then cut back right and downhill. This problem faces downcanyon.

❒ 1. **Tiger Stripes V7** ★★
Stand start on a left-hand sidepull and a right-hand flat edge. Project from low and right.

E. Storm Shadow

Walk around The Kind Traverse Boulder on the right side. Follow a social trail upcanyon for 25 yds to two boulders. Storm Shadow is on the left, The Cube Boulder is on the right.

❒ 1. **Storm Shadow Stand V10** ★★★
Stand start with a right hand on a good edge, left hand on a pinch.
FA Jim Belcer

❒ 2. **Storm Shadow V12** ★★
Sit start down and left on opposing sidepulls. Cross to a pinch, jump out right to a good edge, head straight up.
FA Chris Schulte 2008

F. The Cube Boulder

Just beyond Storm Shadow on the right.

❒ 1. **V6** ★
Squat start on a flat white edge, climb left up the seam.

❒ 2. **V5** ★★
Sit start on a left-facing sidepull, climb the arête.

❒ 3. **V6** ★★★
Stand start on a left-facing sidepull under the roof and a right hand on an undercling.

Tiger Stripes

Storm Shadow

The Cube Boulder

G. The Swing of Things

Facing away from the arête on The Cube Boulder (#2). Walk downhill and right 10 yds. The problem faces upcanyon.

❒ 1. **The Swing of Things V9** ★
Start standing on a sloper and a high left-hand incut sidepull. Head out left. Looks stellar, but climbs less than so. Has not been climbed from lower.
FA Jim Belcer mid 90s

H. Belcer Roof

Facing The Swing of Things, walk right, around a small boulder, to this low roof on the right.

❒ 1. **Belcer Roof V9** ★
Sit start low on underclings, and climb the roof.
FA Jim Belcer mid 90s

I. Kneebar

Just left of the Belcer Roof.

❒ 1. **Kneebar V6** ★★
Start sitting, climb up through good rock and a kneebar.

J. Warm Up Boulder

❒ 1. **Warm Up V1** ★★
Start matched on a flat edge, climb straight up.

K. Edge Boulder

From The Swing of Things, head right to the next large boulder, just a few feet away. Walk around the right side to this obvious face.

❒ 1. **Beginner's Luck V3** ★★★
Start matched on a flat edge, climb up awesome flat edges.

The Swing of Things

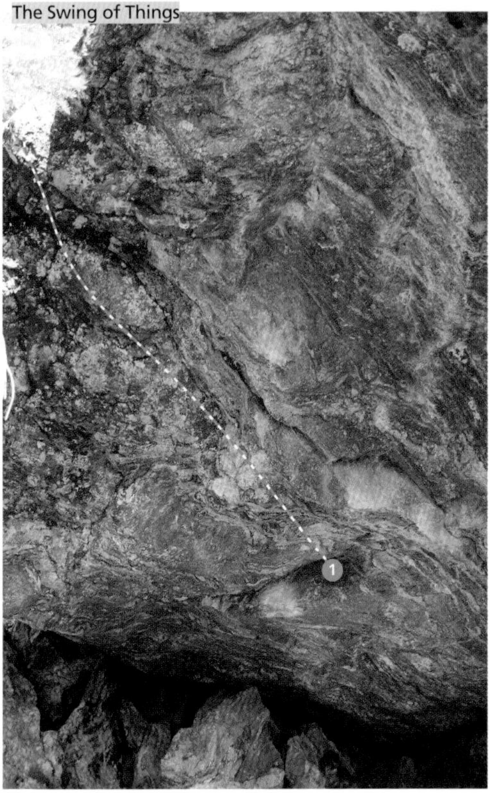

Kneebar

Belcer Roof

Warm Up Boulder

Edge Boulder

L. Brown Frown

From The Cube, head upcanyon 40 yds, parallelling the creek on your right. The path will drop downhill, to the creek, and the Brown Frown is on your left, just a few yards from the creek.

❒ 1. **Brown Frown V8 ***

Start sitting on opposing sidepulls and slap up the compression feature.

FA Adam Strong 2010

Brown Frown

Dave Graham, spotted by Chad Greedy, on Storm Shadow V12. Photo by Caroline Treadway

Large Sector

The Large Boulder sits by itself on the north side of the valley, on the opposite side of the Emerald Lake Trail from The Kind Traverse. From the turn off to the Kind Traverse Sector, continue on the Emerald Lake Trail for 10 yds and hike uphill to the right, following a faint social trail for 30 yds. The boulder is visible from the Emerald Lake Trail.

Large Boulder

A. Large Boulder

❒ 1. **Tommy's Arête V9** ★★
Start sitting, with a left hand low on the arête and a right hand on the lowest sloping edge. Climb the knifeblade arête. Topout for full credit.
FA Tommy Caldwell 2000

❒ 2. **Large V9** ★★★
Start on two underclings. Make a huge move up and right to a plate, then to a bad pinch. Morphological.
FA Hank Jones 1999

❒ 3. **Real Large V9** ★★★
Start matched on a good flat hold. Climb up and right into underclings, move out left to a crimp. Finish.
FA Hank Jones 1999

❒ 4. **Conquest V12** ★★
Start standing high on two poor underclings. Pull on and fire to an edge. Topout.
FA Andre Difelice

❒ 5. **Hi Fi V11** ★
Start sitting and climb right, through poor crimps in the seam. Finish to the right.
FA Harry Robertson 2004

❒ 6. **Arête V8** ★
Start sitting on a blocky incut jug and climb the overhanging feature.

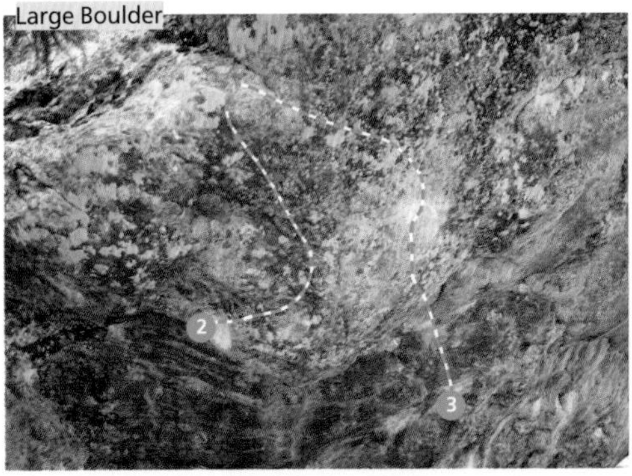

Large Boulder

Large Boulder

Arête

Ryan Olson on the glorious finish of Weeping Willow V10. Photo by Caroline Treadway

Hallett Boulder

The Hallett Boulder offers unequaled scenery, some amazing problems, and a true alpine bouldering experience. The boulder is a solid 40-minute hike past Emerald Lake. A visit is, by bouldering standards, a serious endeavour, and retreat from here is slow and difficult. Be always on the lookout for approaching storms. The elevation of the Hallett Boulder is 10,800 ft.

Season

The Hallett Boulder does not typically melt out until the end of June. It is also one of the first boulders to go under snow, and the short season ends sometime towards the end of September.

Approach

Take the Emerald Lake Trail to the shore of Emerald Lake (elev. 10,100 ft) 1.8 miles from the Bear Lake Parking Lot. Head left around the shore of the lake about 30 yds and cut very steeply uphill on a faint climber's social trail over loose rock. At the top of the plateau head upcanyon over uneven and rocky terrain. There is a hard-to-follow trail, but pick your way over the talus and continue upcanyon, avoiding a large cluster of trees by heading up left and around them.

Past the trees near the base of the 800-ft east face of Hallett Peak (12,713-ft) cross a boulderfield and make your way for several hundred yards very steeply up intermittent polished cliffbands, snow, and patches of tundra for several hundred yards. Pick the path of least resistance, staying just left of the precipitous drop to Tyndall Creek. The triangular shaped Hallett Boulder, which is visible from the shore of Emerald Lake, goes out of view. Eventually this massive boulder will come back into view. Most of the problems face the sprawling, enormous wall of Hallett Peak, and this is a good place to drop your things, 1,350 ft above and 2.1 miles from the Bear Lake Trailhead.

Hallett Boulder

Hallett Boulder

❒ 1. **V6 Arête V6** ★
Start on a good pinch on the right arête, climb the left-leaning arête.

❒ 2. **Keeping It Rail V11** ★★
Start on a good pinch on the right arête, traverse left on flat edges about head 6 ft off the ground, into the end of Fireball. Topout as for Fireball.
FA Tyler Landman 2005

❒ 3. **Fireball V10** ★★
Start crouched on a left-hand flat 3-finger edge and a low right-hand quarter-pad undercling. The first move is to a sharp right-hand pinch. Flip the left hand to a sidepull and fire to a sharp incut hold.
FA David Graham 2003

❒ 4. **Project**
Start low and make some hard compression moves.

❒ 5. **Stanger in a Strange Land V12** ★★★
Start sitting with a right-hand flat crimp and a left-hand rounded undercling. Pull on, cross over to an incut edge and climb up incuts and flat holds. Great steep climbing.
FA David Graham 2003

❒ 6. **Bring the Ruckus V11** ★★★
Start as for Stranger, but head left, through underclings, finishing with a big move.
FA Daniel Woods 2005

Hallett Boulder-Fireball

Hallett Boulder-Stranger in a Strange Land

❒ 7. **V8** ★
Start with a good left-facing edge and an undercling. Climb up and right, following a faint seam.
FA David Graham 2003

❒ 8. **Weeping Willow V10** ★★
Around the corner and to the left of #7. Start sitting down in the hole on a good low jug. Climb up and right, through sidepulls. Avoid the dab coming around the corner and finish up the committing, but jug-filled, rail that heads right over the water. This problem is often unclimbable until August, when the meltwater stream flowing underneath it finally subsides.
FA David Graham 2003

❒ 9. **Fire Crotch V9** ★★
Start low on opposing sidepulls, and climb the overhanging prowlike feature. The first ascent stepped off right, but on the second ascent Daniel Woods topped this problem out, up the huge chossy wall, thinking he was climbing Weeping Willow.
FA Ryan Olson 2005

❒ 10. **The End of the Beginning 5.13b**
The only sport route on the east face of the Hallett Boulder. three bolts and some gear. This can be bouldered out early in the season when the snow is high. Kevin Jorgeson was the first to do so in 2010.
FA Matt Segal 2005

Hallett Boulder-V8

Hallett Boulder-Weeping Willow

Hallett Boulder-The End of the Beginning

Hallett Boulder-Fire Crotch

An elk grazes on the tundra, well above the tree line, as the summer storm clouds build behind it.

Alex Puccio makes a flash ascent of Fireball V10

Golden Ice Boulder

A very nice boulder, just downstream from the massive east face of the Hallett Boulder.

❒ 1. **Golden Ice V7** ★★★★
Start standing in the middle of the face, move up to good pockets and then a good edge, then straight up the face.

Jamie Emerson enjoying perfect weather and excellent rock in Tyndall Gorge, attempting Bring the Ruckus V11. Photo by Ryan Olson

RMNP6 Lower Chaos

Sarah Orens on Gang Bang Arête V8 Photo by Wade David

Lower Chaos Canyon Boulders

This was the first cluster of boulders found by Mike Caldwell and developed mostly by David Graham in the summers of 2000 and 2001. Perfectly polished gneiss, on the shores of Lake Haiyaha, with an excellent collection of hard climbs, make this one of the most popular destinations in Colorado. Longs Peak, the highest point in the Park, looms over the boulderfield. The elevation of Lower Chaos is 10,219 ft.

Season

The boulders in Lower Chaos are climable as early as the beginning of June, and until late October.

Approach

From the Park Entrance on Highway 36, drive 200 yds and turn left onto Bear Lake Road. Take Bear Lake Road for 10.0 miles to the Bear Lake Parking Lot at the end of the road. Park here. It's best to arrive early in the morning or after 3 pm, especially on the weekends (the shuttle bus can be a good option during the busy season). The Bear Lake Parking Lot is a large parking area with one trailhead at its western end.

Hike past the Ranger Station that marks the trailhead (elev. 9,450 ft) and cross a sturdy footbridge into the forest. Turn left, and then take the right fork, passing the Glacier Gorge Junction Trail on your left. The paved path leads uphill into the forest. The

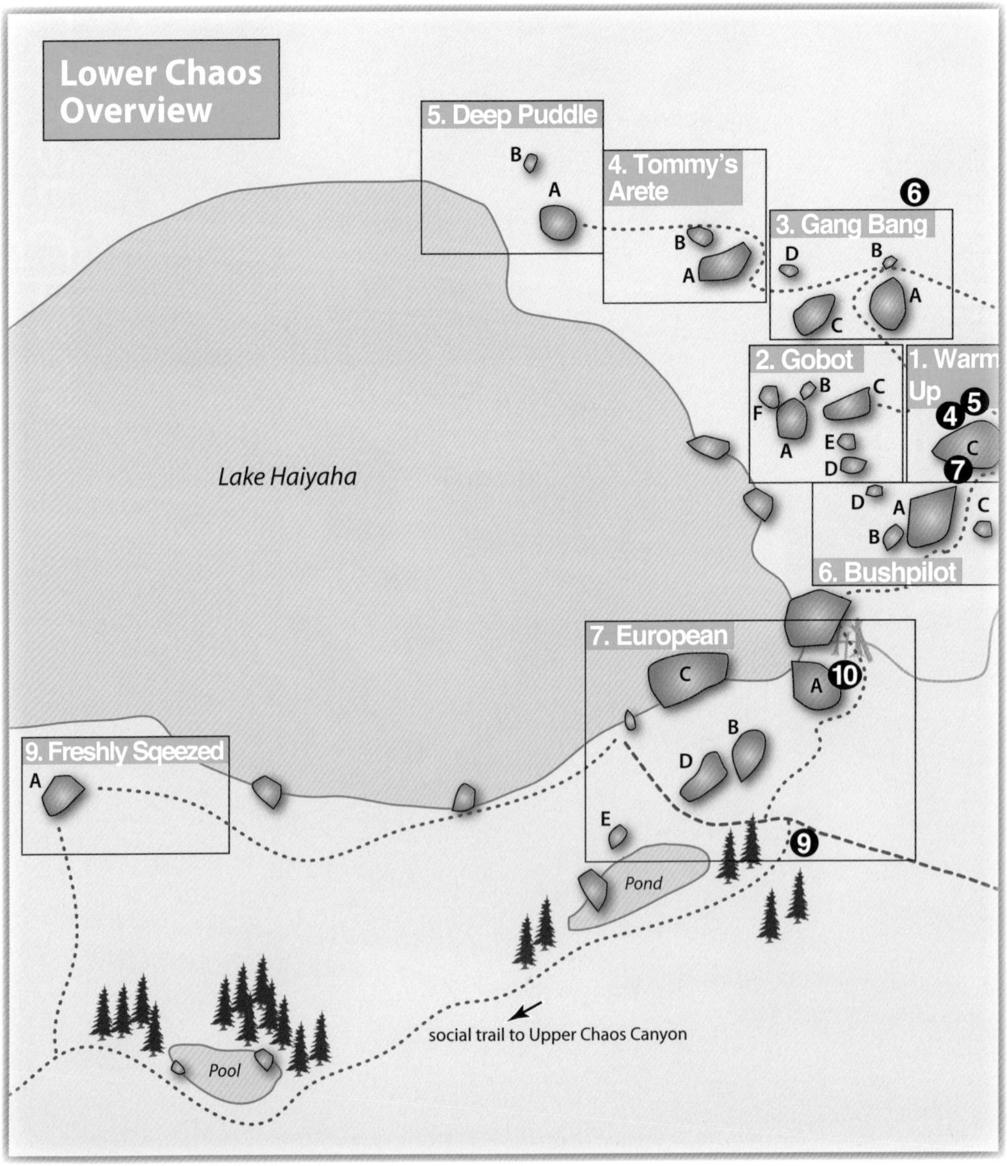

pavement ends near Nymph Lake (elev. 9,700 ft), which appears through the trees at 0.6 miles, on the left. Continue on the trail, around the lake and uphill, to expansive views of Glacier Gorge and Longs Peak (elev. 14,259 ft) the highest point in the Park.

Continue uphill, crossing Tyndall Creek on a footbridge. Soon after the trail levels out there is a junction. Take the left fork, which is the Lake Haiyaha Trail, heading uphill through dense sub-alpine forest. The trail makes a switchback after several hundred yards. In a few hundred yards, the trail bends to the right and the view opens up back down towards Estes Park. At a high point, the trail bends right again around a dead tree and marches downhill. At the bottom of the hill the trail flattens as it bends to the left. From the bend, hike 25 yds to a small clearing on the right and a tree, 1.6 miles from the Bear Lake Parking Lot. A footbridge on the Lake Haiyaha Trail crosses Chaos Creek 10 yds beyond this clearing.

Upper Chaos Canyon

To access Upper Chaos Canyon, continue over the bridge and follow the Lake Haiyaha Trail. (see page 148)

Lower Chaos Canyon

To access Lower Chaos Canyon, from the clearing, head right on a social trail. Follow the social trail through stunted trees, paralleling a pond filled with boulders to the left of the trail. Follow the social trail for 50 yds, then head left out of the trees into the boulder-filled pond. Rock-hop upcanyon 150 yds to the First Warm Up Boulder. For Gang Bang Arete, Tommy's Arete and Deep Puddle Dynamics, there is a direct approach, which continues through the trees on a social trail, and is shown below.

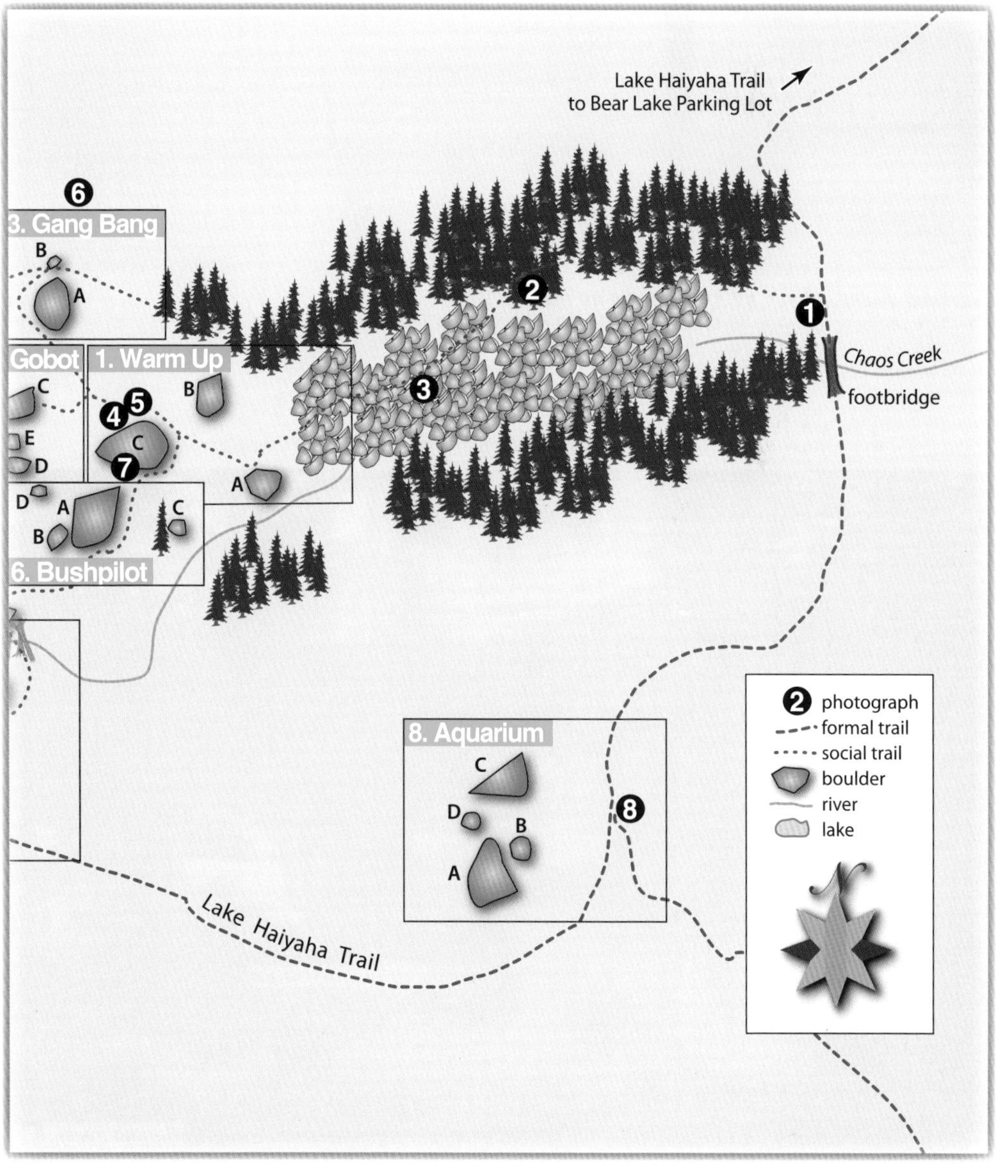

Getting there...Step by step (fork by fork)

The above photo, which marks the beginning of the hike, was taken just beyond the Bear Lake Ranger Station and past a sturdy footbridge. Head left past the bridge, then take the right fork, to Emerald Lake and Lake Haiyaha. Follow the written directions on the previous page towards Lake Haiyaha and eventually to a small clearing and a tree, 1.6 miles from the Bear Lake Ranger Station.

At the small clearing, head right, following a social trail for 100 yds to some logs and a dead tree stump.

At the dead tree stump, head left into the talus and rock-hop for 50 yds to the First Warm Up Boulder. There is no trail here, so find the path of least resistance and pick your way over water and rock.

Warm Up Sector

These boulders are the best place to warm up.

A. First Warm Up Boulder

The first boulder encountered. Moderate warm-ups of mediocre quality.

❒ 1. **Welcome to Chaos V3** ★
Start on good holds at waist height. Move up and left into a shallow dihedral.

❒ 2. **Right V3** ★
Start as #1 and move right on good edges to a tricky topout.

❒ 3. **Warmup Roof V5** ★
Start sitting under a small roof on two crimps. Make a long move to the lip.

B. The Dashboard Boulder

A small boulder with a low roof that faces downcanyon. Just beyond the First Warm Up Boulder on the right.

❒ 1. **Colt 45 V9**
Start squatting on a left edge and a flat right-hand sidepull. Climb the roof. This has broken several times, but still gets V9.
FA Alex DiFelice

❒ 2. **The Dashboard Left V10**
Climb up and left, starting matched on the slopers, then traverse the lip out left.
FA David Graham 2000

❒ 3. **The Dashboard Right V10**
A contrivance. Start matched on a sloping rail, move up and left to a small crimp, and either move left or jump right to a good hold over the lip. The small but good crimp up and right from the slopers in the beginning is off. This problem is also known as Stars and Stripes, which was thought to be a James Litz FA. Using the small crimp up and right of the slopers and climbing the uncontrived version is V8.
FA David Graham 2000

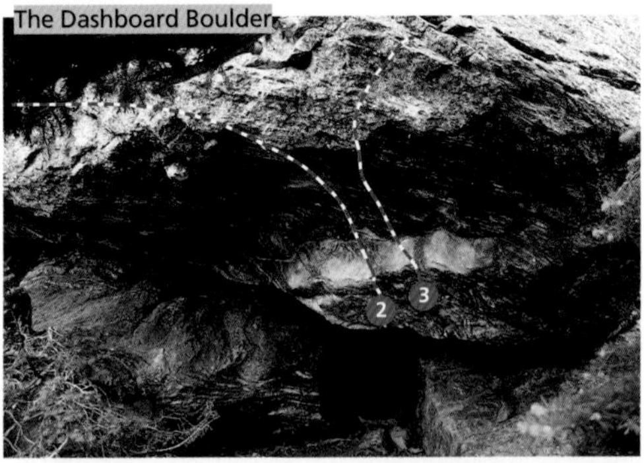

C. The Warm Up Boulder

Walk around the First Warm Up Boulder on the right, passing The Dashboard Boulder on your right. Head straight upcanyon 20 yds. The best place to warm up. Numerous moderate variations exist on this boulder.

❒ 1. **Left V1** ★★
Start crouched on a right-hand sidepull and a poor left-hand and climb straight up the wall.

❒ 2. **Right V3** ★★★
Start matched on a chest-high hold and climb up through a sloper and rib for the left.

❒ 3. **Potato Chip V7** ★★
Start standing at the right side of the face with a left hand on a flat edge and right-hand on a sidepull edge. Cross over to a flat left-hand crimp, move up and right to a razorblade edge, then again to the "potato chip" hold. The end is committing but manageable. The sit start begins to the left on a big left-hand sidepull and a small right-hand crimp. Move straight up, then right into Potato Chip. This is V8.
FA Tommy Caldwell 1999

❒ 4. **Lone Orchestra V7**
Walk up the boulder past Potato Chip to a small boulder that leans up against and faces The Warm Up Boulder. Start sitting on underclings. A problem of poor quality.
FA Harry Robertson 2004

D. Little Orb

Facing The Warm Up Boulder, walk around the left side. The Little Orb is 10 yds down and left.

❒ 1. **Left V1** ★★
Start standing, climb the face.

❒ 2. **Right V1** ★★
Start on the right side, climb the face.

Little Orb

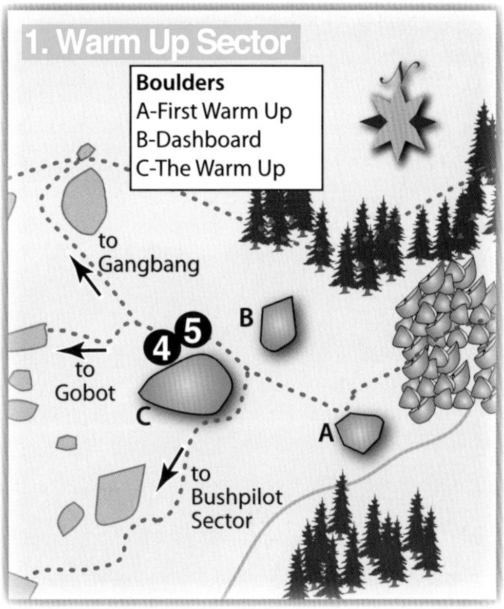

Gobot Sector

This is another great place to warm up, and home to a few Lower Chaos classics. Walk around the right side of The Warm Up Boulder. At the end of the boulder, head slightly left and then straight upcanyon. About 30 yds from The Warm Up Boulder.

Gobot Approach

A. The Gobot Boulder

A classic and intimidating wall with two outstanding problems. From the top of The Gobot Boulder there are good views of Lake Haiyaha.

❒ 1. **The Autobot V5** ★★★
Start down in the slot, matched on a large flat block. Climb straight up on small crimps to a fun layback crack. The sit start (V8) begins sitting at the base of the wall with a left hand on a sidepull undercling and a right hand on a sidepull.

❒ 2. **Slowbot V9** ★★
Start on The Autobot but cut out left after a few moves, and finish on The Gobot.

❒ 3. **The Gobot V11** ★★★
Start standing at the base of the wall, down in the hole, on a good incut edge. Cross over to a flat edge for the left, then a big move out right. Place a heel on the large block and climb straight up the wall, making a massive move to a tooth for the right. Continue directly up the wall. Committing, but manageable with good pads.
FA David Graham 2000

❒ 4. **The Decepticon V10** ★
Start on The Gobot, head left, up the arête, then back right.
FA Nick Sagar 2000

❒ 5. **Offwidth V1** ★
Climb the obvious offwidth crack from a stand start.

B. The Fat Lady Boulder

An odd boulder, just right of The Gobot Boulder.

❒ 1. **Fat Lady V10**
Start standing in the hole, with a left hand on the left arête and a right hand on a white four-finger crystal edge. Climb up the compression feature. Would be outstanding sitting in a meadow, but it's not.
FA David Graham 2000

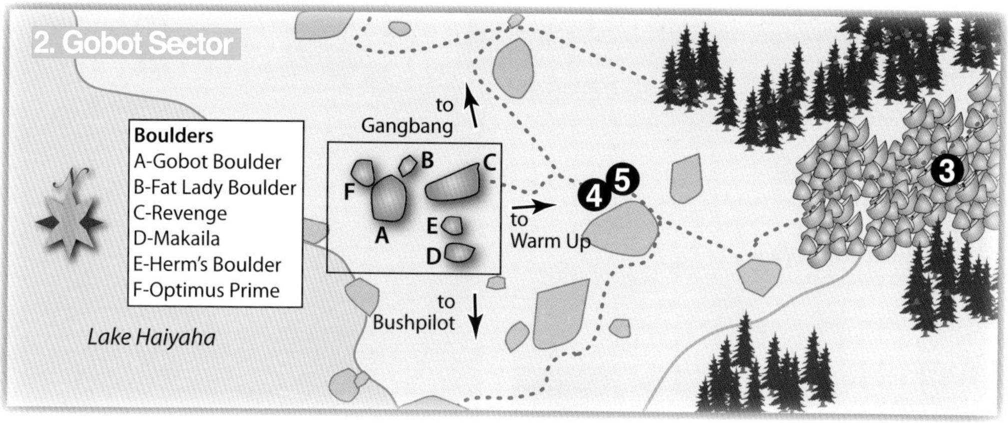

C. Revenge Boulder

A low but popular boulder 5 yds downcanyon from The Gobot Boulder.

❒ 1. **Warm Up V3** ★★
Start sitting, with a left hand on a flat edge, and a right hand on a blocky sidepull. Climb the face on more flat edges.

❒ 2. **Warm Up V1** ★★
Start squatting with a left-hand edge and small, right-hand sidepull. Climb up the edges. Finish right or left. Both exits get the same grade.

❒ 3. **In the Light V8** ★
Start sitting, on underclings, and make a hard first move and head up the crack.
FA Dave Marquess

❒ 4. **Revenge V6** ★★
Start sitting, on the far right side of the wall, with a left hand on an incut crimp and a right hand on a jug sidepull. Climb up the overhanging prow. Josh's "revenge" for failing to do The Marble that day.
FA Josh Heiney 2000

D. Makaila Boulder

Faces the Revenge Boulder.

❒ 1. **Makaila V7** ★★
Start sitting, left hand on a blocky hold, right hand on a crimp and make a hard move, followed by easier climbing.

❒ 2. **Wyoming Chinese V7** ★★
Stand start on two small crimps, cross to a good crimp and head up and right to the arête. Committing.

E. Herm's Boulder

A small roof that faces Makaila.

❒ 1. **Herm's Problem V8** ★
Start sitting with a right-hand pistol grip. Big moves. Germanic.
FA Herman Feissner 2000

F. Optimus Prime

A small boulder. Walk towards Lake Haiyaha from the topout of The Gobot.

❒ 1. **Optimus Prime V9** ★
Start matched on a jug under the roof and climb straight up on small crimps over a horrible landing.
FA David Graham 2000

Got Snow? No Snow? Early Season Problem Suggestions

Lower Chaos and Upper Chaos

Every year the winter snow comes down in copious amounts to bury most of the problems in RMNP. This has its advantages and disadvantages. It can provide a packed and easy pathway over the talus and it can smooth out the nastiest of landings. It can also completely bury many of the classics well into July. Some problems, like Riddles in the Park, go from being buried, to having a perfect snow landing, and then as the snow recedes, a jumbled talus landing. Keep in mind that every year is different, which adds to the adventure!

Problems that benefit in the early season from a snow landing:

Lower Chaos:
The Centaur/Marble V12/11
Deep Puddle Dynamics V9
Optimus Prime V9
The Gobot V11
The Autobot V5

Upper Chaos:
Riddles in the Park V10
Full Chaos V10
Terrorism Arête V7
El Capitan V2-V7 (depending on the time of year)

Problems that are buried (completely) early in the year:

Lower Chaos:
Gang Bang Arête V8
Nuthin' But Sunshine V13
Bushpilot V11 (sometimes this doesn't melt out until August!)

Upper Chaos:
Riddles in the Park V12
Sunspot V10

Gang Bang Sector

The Gang Bang Approach photo shows the view, looking northwest, from the top of The Warm Up Boulder. From The Warm Up Boulder, head upcanyon and slightly right 50 yds. There is not an established path here, but pick your way over the rocks and avoid trampling any vegetation. It is easiest to head left around the trees in the center of the photo.

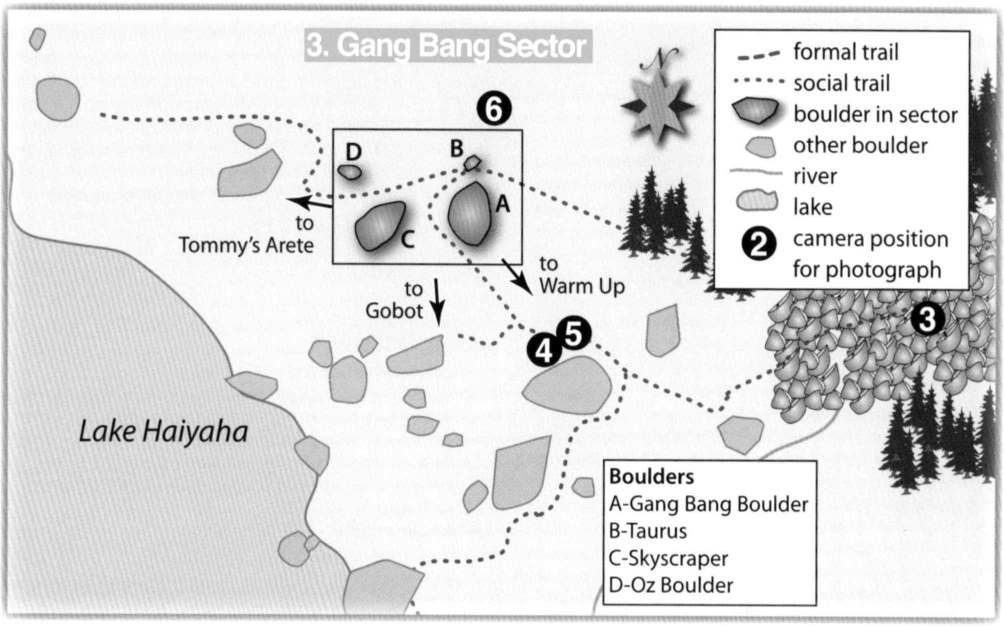

A. The Gang Bang Boulder

One of the most popular boulders in the Park, with loads of good, hard problems.

❒ 1. **Gang Bang Arête V8** ★★
Start crouched with a right-hand pinch and a left hand on the arête. A left-hand pinch leads to hard move to a flat sloper. A diminutive testpiece. This has been campused and climbed with a crashpad.
FA David Graham 2000

❒ 2. **Future Development V10**
Start as Gang Bang Arête, doing the same first move, then head left about 3 feet, moving up to a small, angular crimp and finishing with a big move to a rounded jug.
FA David Graham 2004

❒ 3. **Mezmerizer V11** ★
Start as Gang Bang Arête, head farther left, past Future Development, making a huge right-hand move to a three-finger edge. Finish on Handicapps.
FA Luke "Gomez" Parady 2009

❒ 4. **The Alley V13** ★
Start on Gang Bang Arête and finish on The Marble.
FA Andre DiFelice 2008

❒ 5. **Aslan V14** ★
Start on Gang Bang Arête, finish on The Centaur.
FA Daniel Woods 2006

❒ 6. **Handicapps V9** ★★
Start matched on a flat undercling in the middle of the wall, with a large right foot. Climb up through another undercling, finishing with a tough move out right to a horn.
FA Brian Capps 1999

❒ 7. **Handicapps Arête V9** ★★
Climb Handicapps, but finish up the left-trending arête. Adds a V6 and is often climbed when the snow is high.
FA David Graham 2000

❒ 8. **The Centaur V12** ★
This climb is a contrivance, and to properly complete it the climber must follow a specific set of holds. Start on Handicapps and climb left to a left-angling incut edge. Move through a four-finger slot. Left hand to a pinch, right hand to a fat sidepull. From here climb straight up to two small incut crimps, one for the left hand, one for the right. A high step and a long lock-off to a small chip for the left, and then to the lip. This problem has broken several times.
FA David Graham 2001. Alex Puccio did the FFA in 2010.

❒ 9. **The Marble Sit V11** ★
Start on Handicapps and climb left, through a four-finger slot hold. Go to a pinch with your right hand and move left, taking the path of least resistance to the lip. More traversing in nature than The Centaur.
FA Andy Raether 2003

❒ 10. **The Marble V9** ★
Named for a small marble that was found at the base of the climb. Start matched on a left-angling incut edge. Move left through a four-finger slot and head to the lip taking the path of least resistance. One of the first hard problems in Chaos Canyon. It has broken several times, making it easier than its original grade of V10.
FA Nick Sagar 2000

❒ 11. **Secret Splendour V12** ★★
Start sitting on a left-hand edge and a polished right-hand sidepull. Move up and right to another flat sidepull, left to a poor crimp on the arête and then a hard move to a fat pinch.
FA Tyler Landman 2007

❒ 12. **Nuthin' But Sunshine V13** ★★★
Start sitting with a left hand on a block, right hand on an undercling in a seam. Climb straight up the wall on awesome polished rock. A hard sequence leads to the credit card crimp for the right and a hard move to a sloper. Finish right. This exit is slightly harder than going left, and was the line taken on the FA. Classic.
FA David Graham 2000

❒ 13. **Valis V11** ★★
Start standing on a right-hand sloper and left-hand sloping undercling. Climb straight up.
FA David Graham 2003

❒ 14. **Phallus V12** ★★
Adds one hard move by starting with a right-hand on a sloping undercling. The first move is to the right-hand starting sloper of Valis.
FA Corey French 2006

B. Taurus Boulder

Smallish. When facing Gang Bang Arête, just to the right.

❒ 1. **Taurus V7** ★
Start matched on a left-facing, sloping gaston and move up.

C. Skyscraper Boulder

A gigantic boulder, just uphill and towards the lake from Nuthin' But Sunshine.

❒ 1. **Skyscraper V5** ★★★★

Start standing, matched on a good flat edge in the middle of the face and climb the right side of the enormous face. From the obvious horn, head up and right to the arête. The crux is at the top. Terrifying.

FA Nick Sagar 2000

❒ 2. **Vacationland V5** ★★★

Climb the left side of the massive face, finishing out left.

FA David Graham 2000

D. Oz Boulder

This small boulder lies between The Gang Bang Boulder and Tommy's Arête Boulder. Walk past Taurus, around the right side of a large but slabby boulder for 30 yds.

❒ 1. **Oz Project**

Climbed from a sit start by Daniel Woods at V12, this short problem has broken, and has not been climbed since the break.

Skyscraper Boulder

Oz Boulder

Daniel Woods spots Laura Jade Griffiths on Skyscraper V5

Ty Landman makes a quick ascent of Nuthin' But Sunshine V13. Photo by Caroline Treadway

Tommy's Arête Sector

Just beyond Oz, about 50 yds upcanyon from the Gang Bang Boulder.

A. Tommy's Arête Boulder

❒ 1. **Tommy's Arête V7** ★★★
Start sitting at the base of the overhang matched on an incut slot. Climb straight up the arête on classic moves and good rock. One of the first problems established in Chaos Canyon.
FA Tommy Caldwell 1999

❒ 2. **The Automator V13** ★★
Start on Tommy's Arête, but head left through terrible crimps and a very hard move at the end. "What, ya don't crimp?"
FA David Graham 2000

B. Element of Surprise Boulder

Head right, around Tommy's Arête, then walk towards Lake Haiyaha for 10 yds.

❒ 1. **Element of Surprise V12** ★
Start on a left-hand sidepull and the lower of two flat edges. Climb straight up the wall on very small holds.
FA Tyler Landman 2006

❒ 2. **Running Scared V11** ★
Begin as for Element of Surprise but head right, climbing the line of least resistance, topping out to the right.
FA Daniel Woods 2006

Ana Burgos runs an evening lap on Tommy's Arête V7
Photo by Sam Davis

Deep Puddle Sector

From the Element of Surprise Boulder, head downhill, towards Lake Haiyaha and slightly right 50 yds. The Deep Puddle Dynamics Boulder faces uphill, away from the lake.

A. Deep Puddle Dynamics Boulder

❐ 1. **Deep Puddle Arête V5** ★★
Climb the arête from a sit start.

❐ 2. **Deep Puddle Dynamics V9** ★★
Start on underclings on the left side of the face and move right, then straight up through the middle of the wall on flat slopers. A hard pinch move at the lip is followed by committing, but easier climbing. Head right, then back left topping out near the apex of the overhang. A fun problem, but very contrived.
FA David Graham 2000

❐ 3. **V8** ★★
Start matched on a rounded feature, climb straight up.

B. Satellite Boulder

❐ 1. **Satellite V3** ★
Crimpy face near Deep Puddle.

Deep Puddle Dynamics Boulder

Satellite Boulder

Deep Puddle Dynamics Boulder

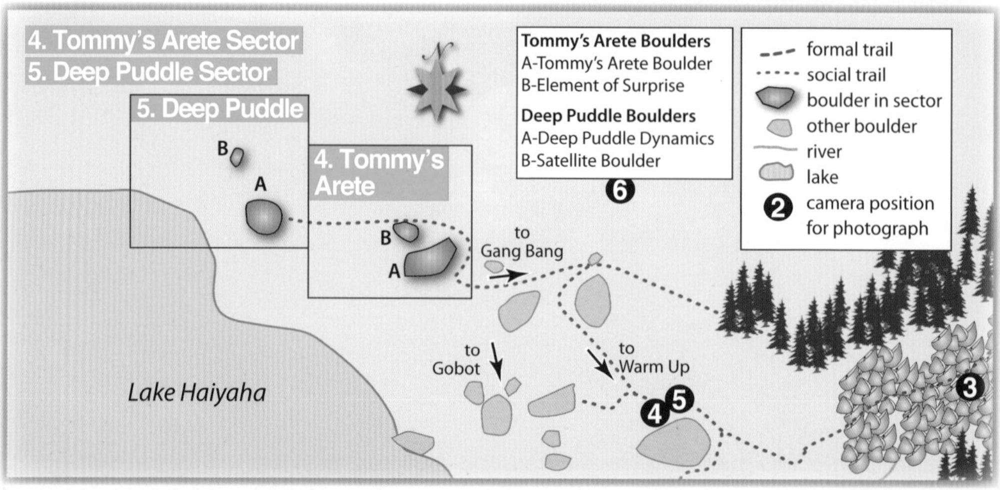

Jason Pinto on Deep Puddle Dynamics V9   Photo by Ryan Olson

Bushpilot Sector

From The Warm Up Boulder, head left around the boulder. Move through some talus heading slightly left. This is the next massive boulder, 10 yds away. The Bushpilot faces away from The Warm Up Boulder. Follow the trail around the left side of the boulder.

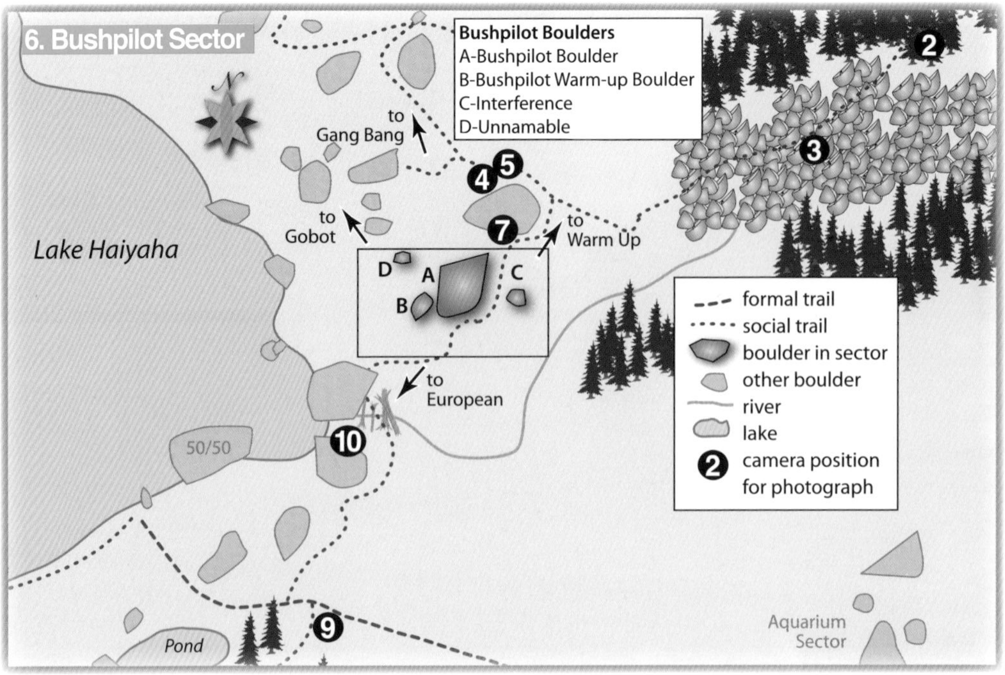

A. Bushpilot Boulder

A massive boulder. All of the problems are hidden from the view of The Warm Up Boulder.

❒ 1. **Bushpilot V11** ★★★

Start sitting at the base of the dihedral, left hand on a pinch on the arête and right hand on a small rounded gaston in the dihedral. Hard compression climbing leads to a difficult move to a flat edge. David Graham has the FA of this classic testpiece, and he originally suggested V10.

FA David Graham 2000

❒ 2. **Freaks of the Industry V13** ★

Start sitting on the same start as Bushpilot. Climb the opening moves in the dihedral, then head right as soon as possible, traversing the wall on small crimps and flat edges. A power endurance testpiece. Technical but straightforward.

FA James Litz 2003

❒ 3. **Freaks and Geeks V8** ★

Start matched on a left-facing sidepull jug and climb straight up, finishing on Freaks of the Industry. Sharp.

B. Bushpilot Warmup Boulder

This boulder is just to the left of Bushpilot.

❒ 1. **V3** ★★★

Start matched on a right facing jug sidepull. Climb the faint crack.

❒ 2. **V6** ★★★

Start on a flat edge and climb straight up the face.

❒ 3. **The Swamp Cooler V6** ★★

Walk back into the cave to the right of #2. Start on a flat edge and climb up and right.

FA Ben Elkon 2009

❒ 4. **Whack Nugget V7**

This small boulder is just right when facing Bushpilot. Start sitting, climb up the slab which faces Freaks of the Industry.

C. Interference

This small problem faces away from The Warm Up Boulder, 7 yds south. From Bushpilot, walk back on a social trail toward The Warm Up Boulder. Interference will be on the right, 20 yds from The Bushpilot Boulder, huddled against a massive pine.

❒ 1. **Interference (Geeks of the Industry) V6** ★
Start sitting on two slot crimps and head straight up the wall, on good rock. Topout right. Originally named Interference.
FA Ted and Stan Lanzano 2000

D. The Unnamable

❒ 1. **Molloy V1** ★★★
Start standing on good edges. Climb incuts to the top. A great warm up.

Seth Allred enjoys a nighttime session on Freaks of the Industry V13. Photo by Caroline Treadway

The Middle Ground

Angela Payne

To me, the Park is all about extremes. From foreign to familiar, frustrating to satisfying and peaceful to turbulent, the Park covers the full spectrum. When I first traveled to this area, I felt more out of place than I ever had in my eighteen years of living. The transition from a chalk-filled gym in the Midwest to the alpine boulderfields of the Rockies was a shock to the system. After my first day of brutal hiking and hopeless flailing, I swore that boulderers in Colorado were out of their minds.

Five years later, I knew the area right down to specific pieces of talus, and I had become one of those crazed boulderers. Certain days in Chaos Canyon were amongst the most frustrating of my life, while others brought me complete satisfaction. At times, the Park is the most tranquil place on Earth. Some of the more peaceful moments of my life were spent lying alone on my crashpad in the Park under a quiet sky full of stars.

But in an instant, the silence can be shattered by a fast-moving alpine storm, and there are more instances than I care to recall when lightning and hail left me running for shelter and swearing to never return to the Park again. But I always do, and always will, because the Park is more than the extremes that it epitomizes. And when I stand in the talus on a perfect fall day surrounded by alpine gneiss and mountain air, I know that the Park can be the perfect middle ground.

In 2008, Angela Payne finally sent her project of three years, the notoriously crimpy and difficult European Human Being V12. Many in the local climbing scene were stunned. Only a handful of women had climbed the V12 grade, and "European" was one of the hardest. Not to be outdone, she set her sights on The Automator V13. This climb gained some note when legendary visiting climbers Malcolm Smith and Jerry Moffatt of the UK and American Chris Sharma tried and failed to thread their way through the small and sloping crimpers. Payne put her singlemindedness and determination to work, and after many days become the first female in the world to climb V13.

Angela Payne climbing the FFA of European Human Being V12. Photo by Caroline Treadway. →

European Sector

From Bushpilot, hike away from the problem up the hill and slightly right, into a mess of trees. Climb up on a boulder that sits in the in lake, walk down to the water. Cross logs and head through the trees. The European Boulder will appear on your right. Fifty yds from Bushpilot (see map page 140).

A. European Boulder

❒ 1. **European Human Being V12** ★★
Start sitting, matched on a flat edge. Move up on terrible crimps. Topout left. A crimping testpiece.
FA Dave Graham 2000 (Angela Payne made the FFA of this stout problem in 2008.)

B. Green Slab Boulder

Walk left around the European Boulder. Climb up the south corner of the European Boulder and look up and right. Walk left from the Green Slab and around the corner to access problems #2–#4.

❒ 1. **Green Slab V1** ★★★
Climb the awesome green slab. The best way is to put a pad on the flat landing zone and climb straight up from here.

❒ 2. **Traverse V3** ★★
Start sitting in a jug slot and traverse right to left on a good flat rail.

Wade David bouldering on the shores of Lake Haiyaha. 50/50 Where it Counts V10. Photo: Wade David Collection

❒ 3. **V4** ★★
Start sitting in a jug slot and climb straight up the wall.

❒ 4. **V10** ★
Start sitting in a jug slot and climb up, then right, on huge moves and flat edges.

C. 50/50 Boulder

Walk right, up a boulder and towards the lake. This massive boulder sits in the lake. Cookie's Corner faces European Human Being, 50/50 Where it Counts is on the opposite side.

❒ 1. **50/50 Where it Counts V10** ★
Stand start, climb the golden face over the flat boulder landing. Numerous holds have broken.
FA Dave Graham 2000

❒ 2. **Cookie's Corner V7** ★★★
Climb the overhanging dihedral early in the season, when the lake is frozen.
FA Mark Hobson 2007

❒ 3. **Project**
An amazing roof project that is rarely climbable due to the high water level of Lake Haiyaha. Interested climbers should show up very early in the season or during a drought.

50/50 Boulder

50/50 Boulder

D. The Cupcake Boulder

This boulder faces #2 and #3 of the Green Slab Boulder.

❐ 1. **The Cupcake V8** ★
Start squatting on two crimps.
FA Blake Rutherford 2005

❐ 2. **Project**
Has not been climbed from a sit start.

❐ 3. **The Gathering Storm V7** ★★
Start standing and climb the faint dihedral.
FA Harry Roberston 2005

E. Pond Boulder

Just left of The Cupcake Boulder is the Lake Haiyaha Trail. Walk over a boulder or two and continue on the Lake Haiyaha Trail past Cupcake. Skirt the north shore of the small pond on the left for 15 yds to a cluster of boulders. The Pond Boulder is a large boulder that faces away from the pond, towards Lake Haiyaha.

❐ 1. **V7** ★★
Start sitting, matched on a low crimp and climb up small and sharp edges.

❐ 2. **V5** ★★
Start sitting, matched on a crimp. Make a move to the crack and traverse right to easier climbing.

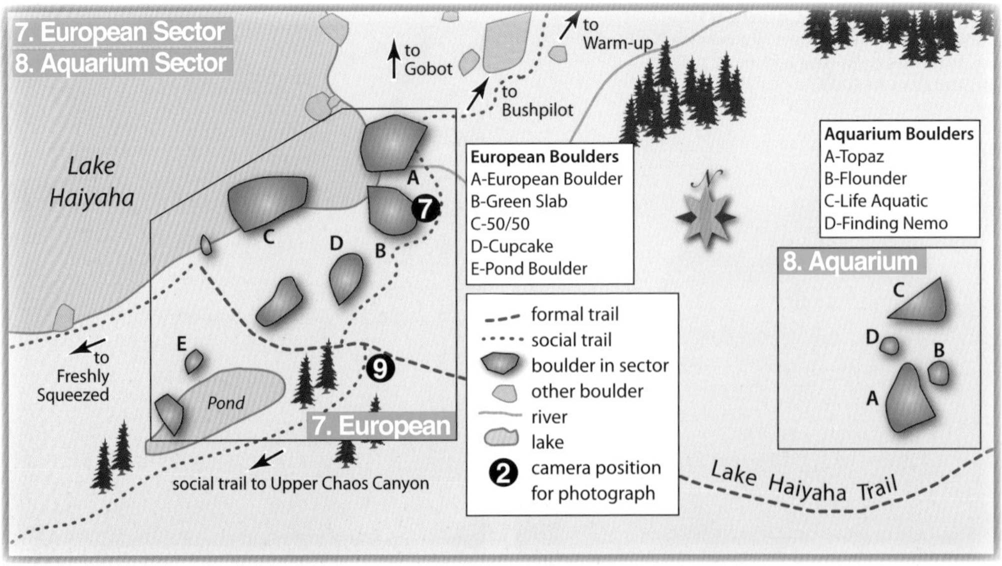

SCARPA
Feroce
THE FEROCE CLIMBING SHOE
UPSIDE DOWN,
RIGHT SIDE UP.
SAME DIFFERENCE.
WHETHER FOR STEEPS,
POCKETS, OR THIN CRACKS,
DEMAND THE MOST FROM YOUR
SHOES. DEMAND FEROCE.
WWW.SCARPA.COM
SCARPA
NO PLACE TOO FAR™

The Aquarium Sector

From the cutoff to Lower Chaos, continue on the Lake Haiyaha Trail past the footbridge over Chaos Creek for 100 yds to the Loch-Mills Trail Junction. Beyond the trail junction 5 yds is a social trail that heads into a cluster of boulders. Follow a faint social trail 25 yds off the right side of the trail into a small cluster of boulders. This is an obscure area, with a few interesting problems, and a great place to climb if you'd like to avoid the crowds in Lower Chaos.

Loch-Mills Trail Jct.

Getting There 8

A. Topaz

This is the largest boulder in the cluster. This boulder faces the Lake Haiyaha Trail.

❒ 1. **Topaz V2** ★★
Start standing on jugs and climb up and right. A gem of the Park.

❒ 2. **The Aquarium Project**
Start standing and climb the direct line up the middle of the face. All of the moves have been done on a toprope. A beautiful but committing line, to say the least.

❒ 3. **Left Line V7**★
Start matched on a flat head-height edge. Head up and left through featured rock.

Topaz

B. Flounder

Flounder faces the large overhanging face of Topaz.

❒ 1. **The Flounder V7** ★
Start sitting on underclings. Climb the small compression feature.

Flounder

C. The Life Aquatic Boulder

Facing Topaz, this boulder is right, 10 yds away.

❒ 1. **The Life Aquatic V10** ★
Start sitting on a left-hand edge and a small, incut, right-hand sidpull. Climb up and right.

❒ 2. **Steve Zissou V11** ★
Start sitting on left-hand edge and a small, incut, right-hand sidepull. Climb up and then left.

D. Finding Nemo

Just upcanyon and in between Topaz and The Life Aquatic.

❒ 1. **Finding Nemo V6** ★
Start standing on a left-hand sidepull and a right-hand undercling. A technical gem.

The Life Aquatic

Finding Nemo

Freshly Squeezed Sector

A. Freshly Squeezed Boulder

Set apart from the rest of Lower Chaos, this is a classic and puissant roof on the shore of Lake Haiyaha. One of the most difficult problems in RMNP to find. There are two approaches. The first hikes around the left (southern) shore of the lake from where the Lake Haiyaha Trail dead-ends at Lake Haiyaha. The problem is about 150 yds from where the trail dead ends, about 20 yds from the shore of the lake. The other approach, which is used more often, follows directions to Upper Chaos. Just past a small pool, cut back right towards the lake for 75 yds. Pick your way over talus and through the trees. Freshly Squeezed faces away from the lake.

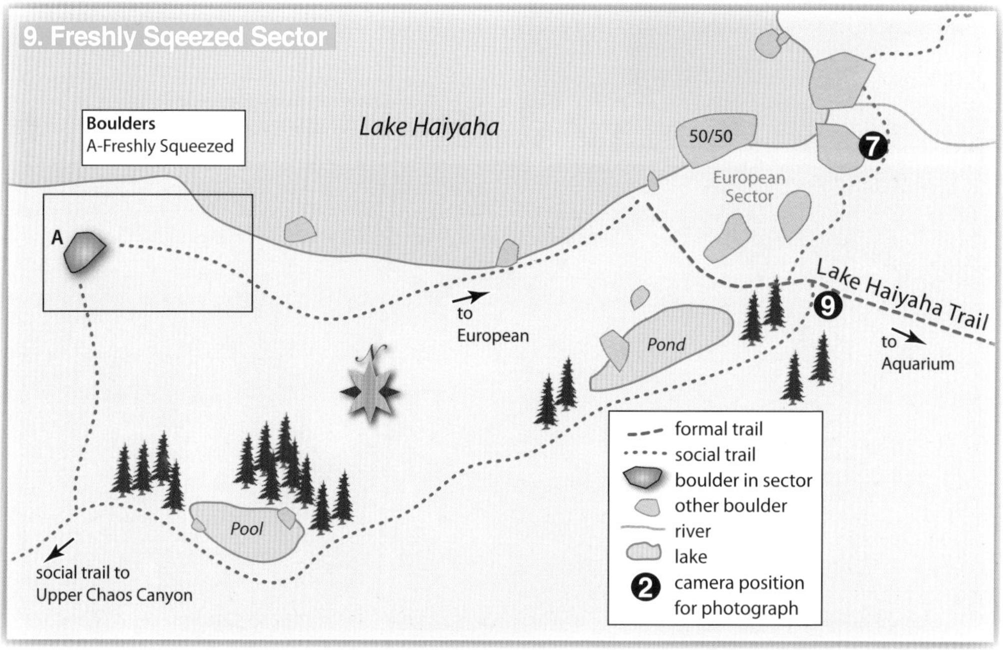

❒ 1. **Freshly Squeezed V12** ★★
Stand start with a right hand low on the arête and a small left-hand crimp/undercling. Climb out the roof on incuts. Awesome tension climbing. David Graham did the first ascent in about an hour, suggesting V10 or V11. Now considered hard for V12. This has been incorrectly referred to as "Freak of Nature."
FA David Graham 2000

Ty Landman on Freshly Squeezed V12
Photo by Caroline Treadway

RMNP7 Upper Chaos

Daniel Woods on the terrifying finish of Suicide Season V7. Photo by Caroline Treadway

Full Chaos
The Pillar
Triple Threat Arête

Green Arête
Lake Haiyaha

Upper Chaos Canyon

Set just below the tree line amongst an infinity of jumbled boulders and a backdrop of stark rock walls, Upper Chaos Canyon is one of the most beautiful and austere climbing areas in the country. The approach is long and complex, and retreat from the vicious storms that come in the summer is difficult. Many of the best hard problems lie hidden and the motivated and intrepid climber will find outstanding steep climbing on excellent rock. The elevation of the meadow in Upper Chaos is 10,508 ft.

Season

The boulders in Upper Chaos Canyon collect a copious amount of snow. If visiting before June, don't expect too much to be climbable. Each season varies. The season typically ends here around the end of September or the beginning of October, with the first few snowfalls.

Approach

There are almost no established trails in Upper Chaos. Most of the time the boulders will be approached by rock-hopping or scrambling over literally thousands of boulders. You can always get from one sector to another by talus hopping in any direction. While this allows for a certain level of freedom, it also makes describing approaches difficult. Take some time to familiarize yourself with the complexity of the area. Retreat from here during a storm is difficult and dangerous, especially if you are unfamliar with the talus field. The black and white numbered circles which appear at the bottom of each photograph correspond to a number on the map to help the climber visiting for the first time. From the trail junction to Lower Chaos continue on the Lake Haiyaha Trail 10 yds, passing over a footbridge and into the forest. After crossing a small stream you will soon come to another trail junction (this cutoff heads left to Glacier Gorge).

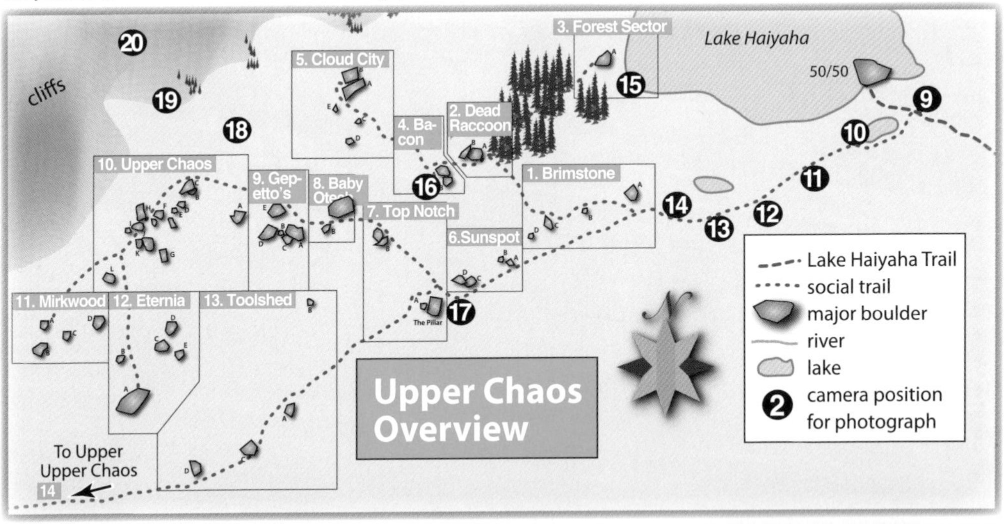

Trail junction on the Lake Haiyaha Trail to Glacier Gorge Parking Area

Continue straight on the Lake Haiyaha Trail, heading slightly uphill for 300 yds. When the trail flattens, just before a seasonal small pond, follow a social trail (see photo #9, below) into the woods on the left. (If you wish to visit Lake Haiyaha, which is a pleasant and spectacular stop on its own, stay on the main trail for 20 yds to the lake shore, where the trail dead-ends.)

Skirt the left shore of the pond through the trees, where the trail is hard to follow. Parallel the shore of the pond as a guideline, picking up the more well-defined social trail on the opposite side of the pond. Head up and slightly left into the boulders, following a faint drainage.

Rock-hop 150 yds (photo #11, above). The drainage will disappear yet the path continues over the boulders. The boulders come to an abrupt end. Emerge from the rock-hop near the reappearance of the social trail and, down on the right, a pool (see photo #12, below).

From here, head upcanyon following the social trail over a section that is usually wet. The views open up (as in photo #13, above) and the trail disappears among the rocks and slabs. From here the trail diverges as shown below.
To reach Brimstone, the Dead Raccoon, the Bacon Wall and The Green 45, follow along in the book from here.
To reach Sunspot, and the rest of Upper Chaos (starting on page 167), continue left up the slabs, staying to the left of the main talus field. The social trail picks up again and heads uphill.

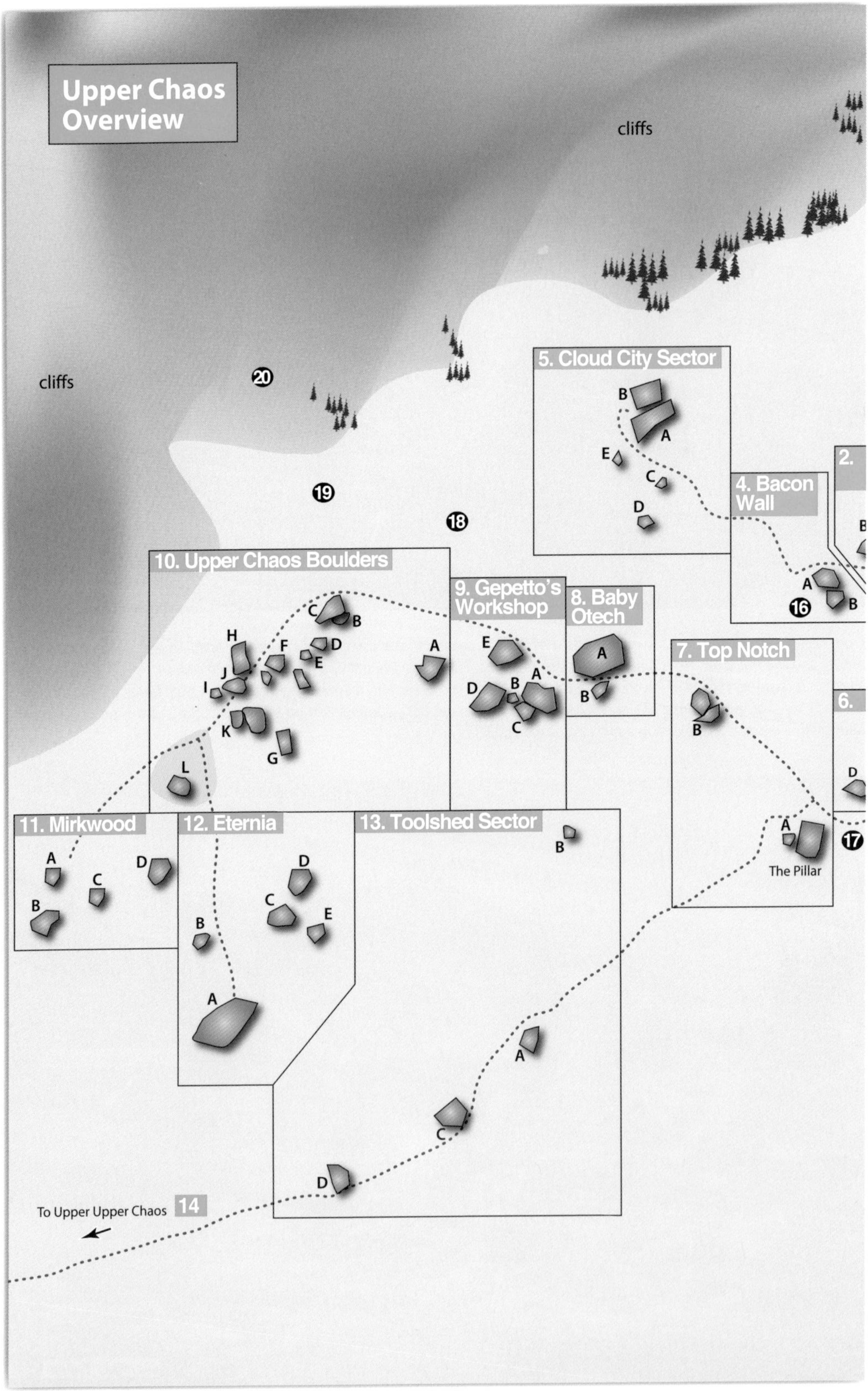
Upper Chaos Overview
cliffs
cliffs
20
19
18
5. Cloud City Sector
B
A
E
C
D
4. Bacon Wall
A
B
16
2.
B
10. Upper Chaos Boulders
C
B
H
F
D
E
J
I
K
G
L
A
9. Gepetto's Workshop
E
A
D
B
C
8. Baby Otech
A
B
7. Top Notch
B
A
The Pillar
17
6.
D
11. Mirkwood
A
C
D
B
12. Eternia
D
C
E
B
A
13. Toolshed Sector
B
A
C
D
To Upper Upper Chaos
14

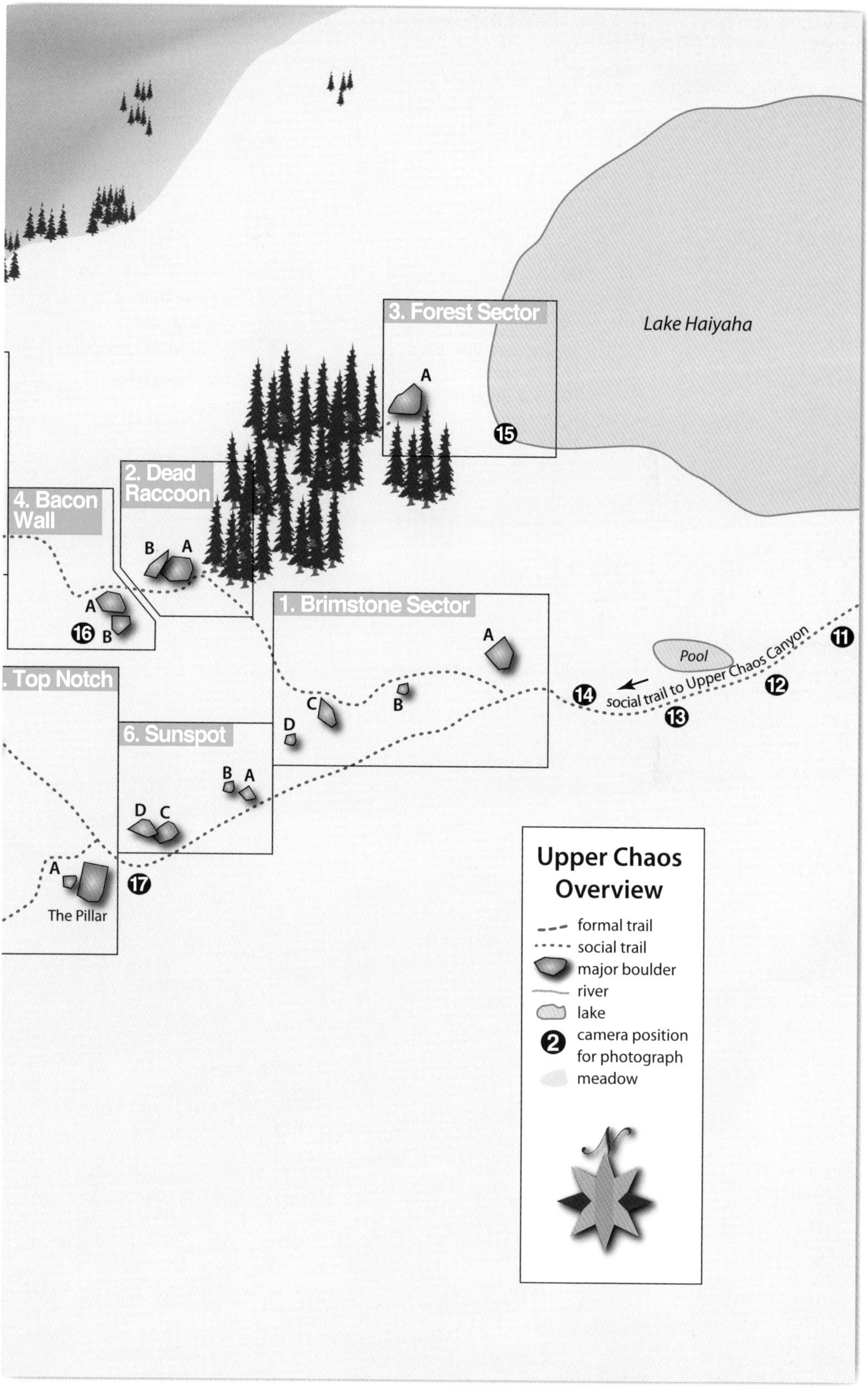

3. Forest Sector
A
15
Lake Haiyaha
2. Dead Raccoon
B
A
4. Bacon Wall
A
16
B
1. Brimstone Sector
A
Pool
11
social trail to Upper Chaos Canyon
12
14
13
C
B
D
. Top Notch
6. Sunspot
B
A
D
C
A
17
The Pillar
Upper Chaos Overview
formal trail
social trail
major boulder
river
lake
camera position for photograph
meadow

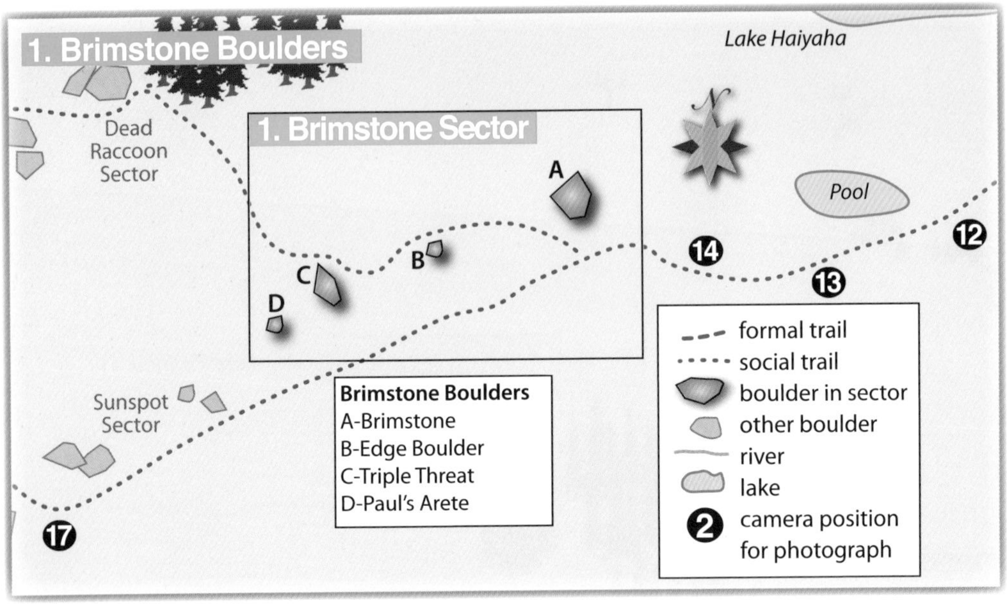

Brimstone Sector

After passing the pool on the right, follow the social trail uphill to some rock slabs. Head right, off-trail, 25 yds into the talus. Brimstone faces uphill.

A. Brimstone

This boulder has two gorgeous slab problems. It faces upcanyon and sits just beyond a large, chossy boulder.

❐ 1. **Brimstone V6** ★★★
Stand start on a right-facing sidepull, climb up the face, staying left on the face.
FA Adam Osterhoff 2000

❐ 2. **V7** ★★★
Stand start on a good rounded edge, climb up the face, following the faint seam.

B. Edge Boulder

Uphill 50 yds from Brimstone, just before Triple Threat. Buried with snow until the middle of July.

❐ 1. **Edges V3** ★★
Start standing on a small crecent-shaped sloping edge. Move up to a good edge, then top out.

C. Triple Threat

This long boulder has one problem on an interesting overhanging feature. Upcanyon 100 yds from Brimstone.

❐ 1. **Triple Threat Arête V10** ★★★
Stand start with a left hand on a small crimp and a right hand on the far right side of the sloping rail feature. One hard squeeze move leads to easier climbing. In early summer this is much less committing when snow fills in the hole to the left.
FA David Graham 2001

D. Paul's Arête Boulder

❐ 1. **Paul's Arête V5** ★★
Just uphill from Triple Threat, near a huge spire-shaped boulder, is this great little arête climb. Stand start. Climb the arête.
FA Paul Otis 2003

Bouldering Development in Chaos Canyon — A Brief Historical Perspective

Brian Capps

It is difficult to argue that Chaos Canyon has not earned its reputation as an international bouldering destination. Some observers might note the abundance and concentration of challenging boulder problems, others are more inclined to recognize the rarely matched beauty of the boulder field and its surroundings, and certainly few visitors fail to recognize that the area provides some of the finest summer bouldering conditions on the continent. These are just a few of the reasons why Chaos Canyon has taken its rightful place among the best bouldering areas in the country. However, the idea that Chaos Canyon would become such a popular bouldering destination would have seemed improbable to many of its early developers.

The potential for a significant number of quality boulder problems within Chaos Canyon was initially unclear, and the vast number of relatively challenging problems it would provide over the following decade was unimaginable. The first season of major bouldering development in Chaos Canyon was cut short due to a late season start. Nevertheless, the first year yielded a number of boulder problems up to V9. It was not until the second year, with a significant amount of help from a young, strong, and extremely motivated Dave Graham, that more difficult boulder problems such as The Automator and The Centaur were established. In addition, much of the new development seemed to spread from lines that had already been climbed, instead of stretching out first to the highest quality, undone lines. For example, Fat Lady, a problem of lesser quality, was established before problems like Bush Pilot simply because of the former's proximity to Autobot, which had been established early on; and it was not until the third year before many considered spending a significant amount of time hiking above The Green 45 Wall (which later produced Jade).

Furthermore, to help put things into perspective, there were few boulder problems in the United States in the year 2000 that had been proposed to be V13 or harder, which only complicated an early evaluation of Chaos Canyon and its newly established problems. One project in Chaos Canyon in particular, dubbed Mission Impossible at the time, had been tried by many locals, was considered by all to be extremely difficult, and was thought to be around V11. After it was established and renamed Nuthin' But Sunshine, it was given V14, a number many of the local developers were unable or unwilling to attach to a climb at the time.

Still other aspects of the climbing culture precluded the early developers from being able to clearly foresee the future status of Chaos Canyon and the bouldering in Rocky Mountain National Park as an international destination. For instance, if you were a typical climber or boulderer in the mid-1990s, there were several things of which you were fairly certain — summers were for climbing on a rope, long approaches were for alpinists or traditional climbers, and uneven rocky landings were for anything other than bouldering over. During the first season or two in Chaos Canyon, many developers were doubtful of whether or not climbers would hike two miles to go bouldering, if a serious climber would forgo a summer of sport climbing in Rifle, Colorado for alpine boulders, or if anyone would be willing to climb over the rocky, uneven landings (remember, at the time, many of the popular bouldering areas in Colorado's Front Range, such as Flagstaff Mountain, Horsetooth Reservoir, Morrison, and Carter Lake were only a short distance from the car and typically involved bouldering over flat landings). Even today, after a decade of bouldering in alpine environments such as those found in Rocky Mountain National Park, some misguided individuals still believe that an approach to an alpine granite area through one of the most beautiful National Parks in the country actually takes away from the quality of the boulder problems in the area.

The next time you find yourself in Chaos Canyon, consider how the area might have appeared to its initial developers. Assuming that you had never climbed in or over a talus field, and that you had never hiked more than one mile to go bouldering, how would you perceive your first visit to Chaos Canyon, and how might you have gone about first developing the area? While questions concerning whether or not climbers would hike miles to go bouldering over an uneven landing have come and gone, the question about how you might begin to establish an alpine bouldering area is more than rhetorical. Right now, in Colorado, there is an undeveloped bouldering area waiting to be discovered. Ten years from now, in a guidebook about this newly discovered boulderfield, I would enjoy reading about some of the issues you uncovered during the first few years of its development.

Dead Raccoon Sector

This massive boulder sits on the north side of Chaos Canyon near a small wooded section. The Forest Sector (page 160) is in the woods just downhill. Head towards Triple Threat and cut right, passing a huge boulder with a large east-facing slab on your left. The Dead Raccoon boulder will soon come into view, uphill and to the left.

A. Dead Raccoon

This is a giant boulder nestled in the trees. The problems face uphill towards the trees, away from the approaching climber.

❒ 1. **What's Left of the Dead Raccoon V7** ★
Start matched on the "tufa-like" pinch, facing uphill and holding the pinch as an undercling. Finish out left, taking the path of least resistance.
FA Jamie Emerson 2007

❒ 2. **Raccoon Turd V8** ★
Start matched on the "tufa-like" pinch, facing uphill and holding the pinch as an undercling. Move left, then back right.

❒ 3. **Dead Raccoon V11** ★★★
Start left hand on a "tufa-like" pinch, right hand on a sloping hold underneath. Move to a sloping edge, then again to dual flat edges, match, and then climb into the compression feature.
FA David Graham 2005

❒ 4. **Project**
Begin on Dead Raccoon, and head right into Hydrotwist.

❒ 5. **Hydrotwist V9** ★★
Stand start on an obvious flat sloper, right of Dead Raccoon and climb up the arête feature, topping out up the dihedral. Scary without snow.
FA David Graham 2005

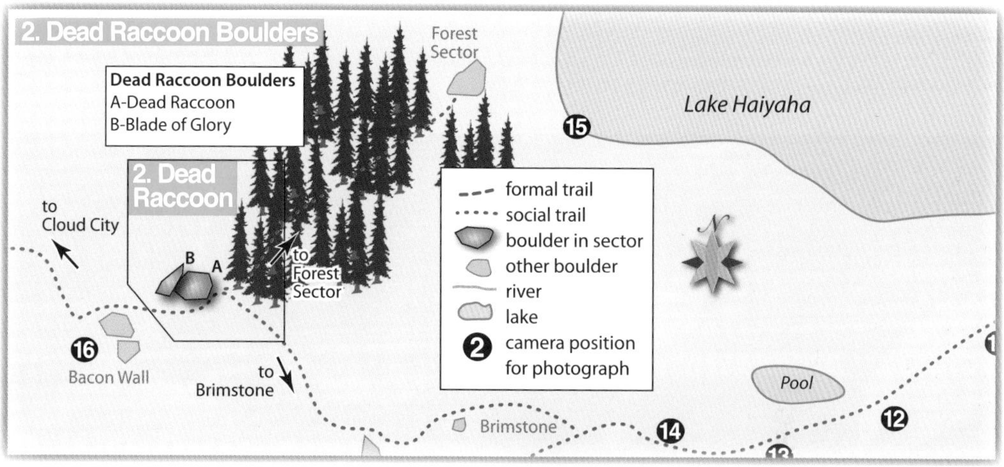

B. Blade of Glory

❒ 5. **Blade of Glory V7** ★★★
Just uphill from Dead Raccoon. Climb the striking arête from a stand start. Chad Greedy got the first ascent of this proud line and worked it on toprope before committing to a ropeless ascent. Very tall.
FA Chad Greedy 2009

❒ 6. **Gomez's Face V7** ★
Climb the face to the right of Blade of Glory from a stand start, finishing out right, over the rock.
FA Luke Parady 2009

Jon Cardwell sends Dead Raccoon V11. Photo by Wade David.

Forest Sector

The Forest Sector lies in the woods on the west side of Lake Haiyaha. From Dead Raccoon hike 150 yds straight downhill into the woods. The massive roof of Forest Boulder lies hidden in the trees and faces Lake Haiyaha.

The other approach is from Freshly Squeezed, in Lower Chaos. From Freshly Squeezed, hike around the southwest shore of Lake Haiyaha. Just before the boulders pictured below cut left, uphill, for 75 yds. To get to the Bacon Wall and Cloud City from here, return to Dead Raccoon and follow the directions on the facing page.

A. Forest Boulder

❒ 1. **Project**
An enormous roof lies hidden in the trees near the lake. This is a contender for one of the hardest projects in America. An imposing boulder. An easier stand start awaits.

❒ 2. **Project**
Climb the left arête of the massive overhang.

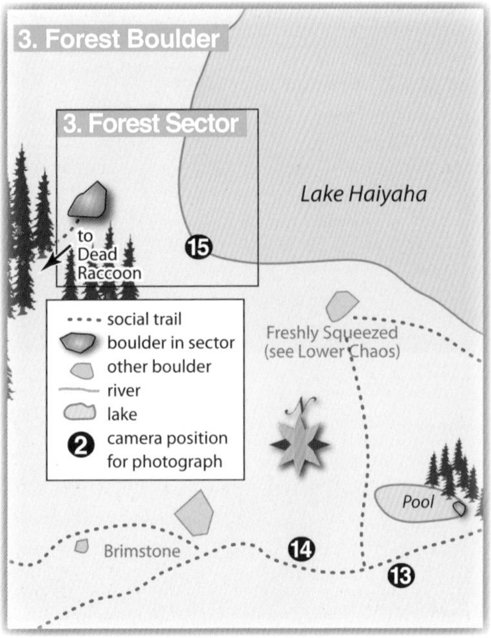

Bacon Wall Sector

Facing Dead Raccoon, hike around the boulder to the left. Head steeply upcanyon, about 50 yds, to a large overhanging face, the Green Arête Boulder. This small cluster has a couple of nice easier problems, and is the best place from which to approach the Cloud City Sector and Jade.

A. Green Arête Boulder

This undercut boulder sits on the edge of a plateau, 20 yds upcanyon from the Dead Raccoon.

❒ 1. **Green Arête V8** ★
Start standing and climb the bold arête.
FA David Graham 2001

❒ 2. **Double Roof V6** ★★
Start low, underneath the roof on a left-hand pinch and a right-hand flat sidepull. Climb straight out the double roof. feature to a mantel.

B. Bacon Wall

This aesthetic boulder is just to the right, when facing Double Roof.

❒ 1. **Bacon Wall V2** ★★
Start matched high on a good hold on white rock and climb straight up the middle of the face.

❒ 2. **V2** ★
Start matched on a big jug on the arête and climb straight up. Beware loose holds near the top.

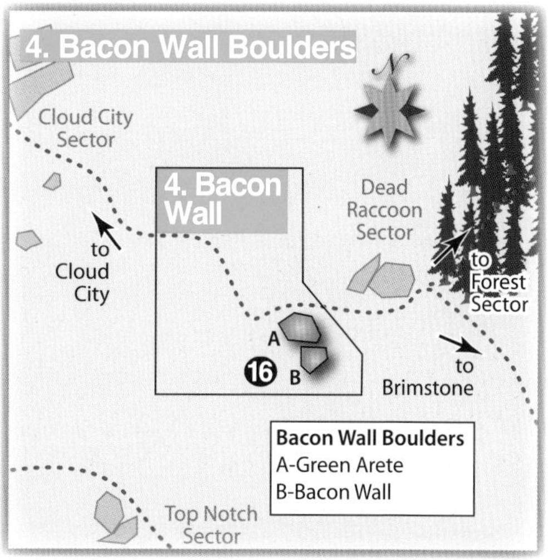

Cloud City

This amazing sector is worth the hike for its excellent concentration of hard problems and wonderful view. It's also home to one of the hardest problems in America.

Cloud City is best approached from the Bacon Wall. The photo below shows the view from Bacon Wall. Hike around to the right of a massive boulder, into a small basin, then head steeply uphill.

Cloud City can also be approached from the Meadow Boulder, which is described on page 171. From the Meadow Boulder, look for the enormous boulders up on a shelf on the north side of the canyon and head straight for them, picking a line of least resistance through the talus. Approaching this way, the Cloud City sector is hidden from view until the last moment, though it is visible from most of the canyon.

View of Cloud City from the Bacon Wall

Otis Peak (elev. 12,484ft) from Cloud City. Typical of the ever-changing weather conditions in Upper Chaos.

A. The Green 45

❒ 1. **Jade V14** ★★★
Start sitting on two small crimps with a right heel hook on a good incut. Move up to a very small right-hand hold. Make "The Move" out left to a small left-hand slot crimp. Climb straight up the wall and topout. Beware of the loose jugs up high. This was one of the most coveted projects in Colorado, and the first problem in the state suggested to be V15. The long standing Green 45 Project.
FA Daniel Woods 2007

❒ 2. **Green 45 Stand V10** ★★
Stand start, right hand on a sharp right-hand sidepull, left hand on a small slot crimp. Make a hard move up and left.
FA David Graham 2001

❒ 3. **1000 Shades of Green V9** ★★
Stand start on opposing bad holds. A hard move to a sharp sidepull leads to a finish up and right on loose jugs.
FA Johnny Goicoechea

❒ 4. **Project**
In 2007 Daniel Woods did all the moves on this very difficult line.

❒ 5. **Don't Get too Greedy V13** ★★★
Start sitting, right hand on a good sidepull jug, left hand on the arête. Move the left hand up and then to a sharp undercling. Continue, climbing the obvious prow. A jump start was done originally at V6, and called La Reve De Wills.
FA Paul Robinson 2007

❒ 6. **Wildcat V11** ★★
On the back side of The Green 45. Crawl through the hole underneath Jade and turn around. Start down and left, left hand in a hole and right hand on an edge out right. Move the left hand up to a good flat edge, and follow a line of holds out right. High in the grade. Imperial.
FA Nick Sherman 2007

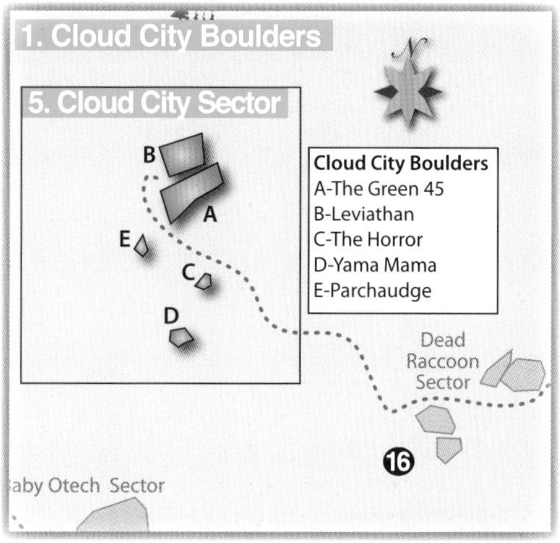

B. Leviathan Boulder

This gigantic boulder sits just behind The Green 45. A low roof overhangs the upcanyon side.

❒ 1. **Two Ton Tongue V10** ★
Start sitting on a flat undercling, low in the roof. Move to an edge, then to better underclings and out the overhang. Establish on the slab and step off to the right. This has been topped out by a few subsequent ascentionists, although the rock is brittle and the landing poor.
FA Seth Allred 2007

❒ 2. **The Loch Ness Monster** V12 ★
Start sitting in the back of the cave, matched on a fingerlock and do a couple of moves into Two Ton Tongue.
FA Daniel Woods 2007

❒ 3. **Leviathan Style V12** ★★
Stand start on good underclings. Climb out the roof, heading slightly left to a large crack. The low start remains a project.
FA David Graham 2001

On the opposite side of the boulder from the roof is a huge vertical face.

❒ 4. **Suicide Season V7** ★★
Start standing, in the bottom of the hole and climb up the huge face. Basically a free-solo. The crux is down low, followed by 5.10 climbing over an un-padable landing. 30-ft tall.
FA Chad Greedy 2002

"I PULLED ON AND ENTERED A ZONE THAT I RARELY VISIT. I WAS UNDER SEA FLOATING TOWARDS THE SURFACE. I EXECUTED THE MOVE — THE MOVE THAT HAD TAKEN ME SIX DAYS OVER THREE YEARS. DON'T FALL NOW, YOU CAN'T FALL NOW... "
TY LANDMAN WRITING ON THE MOON BLOG ABOUT THE SECOND ASCENT OF JADE (V15), ROCKY MOUNTAIN NATIONAL PARK, COLORADO
PHOTO CAROLINE
moon
MOON
TY LANDMAN
JADE (V15)
ROCKY MOUNTAIN
100% CLIMBING
CLOTHING AND HARD GOODS NOW DELIVERED DIRECT FROM THE USA
VISIT: WWW.MOONCLIMBING.COM

C. The Horror Boulder

Forty yards downhill from The Green 45, on a small ridge is the short overhang, which faces towards Lake Haiyaha.

❒ 1. **The Horror V8** ★★

Start matched on a flat edge. Beware the hole. Good rock.
FA Ryan Silven 2009

D. Yama Mama Boulder

Seventy-five yards from The Green 45, this problem lies downhill in the bottom of a small basin that is usually filled with snow until the fall. Yamma Mamma faces away from The Green 45.

❒ 1. **Yama Mama V10** ★★

Start on good edges at the base of the wall, on the lower level. Make a very hard move off the ground and climb incuts, stepping left over a platform landing.
FA Ben Safdi 2005

E. Parchaudge Boulder

Facing Jade, head downhill to the right, to a cluster of large boulders. Parchaudge is about 50 yds from Jade, and faces towards the middle of the canyon.

❒ 1. **Parchaudge V6** ★★

Start sitting at the base of the arête. Climb straight up.
FA David Graham 2008

Sunspot Sector

For climbers wishing to visit Sunspot and the rest of Upper Chaos, follow along in the book from here. Passing the Brimstone Sector on the right, continue on the social trail somewhat left and over rocks. The trail disappears, then picks up again after a small rock slab. Continue heading uphill where the social trail reappears over rocky tundra, with the main boulderfield on your right, heading for The Pillar, an important landmark in Upper Chaos. The Sunspot Sector, Top Notch Sector, and Baby Otech Sector are sometimes referred to as Middle Chaos.

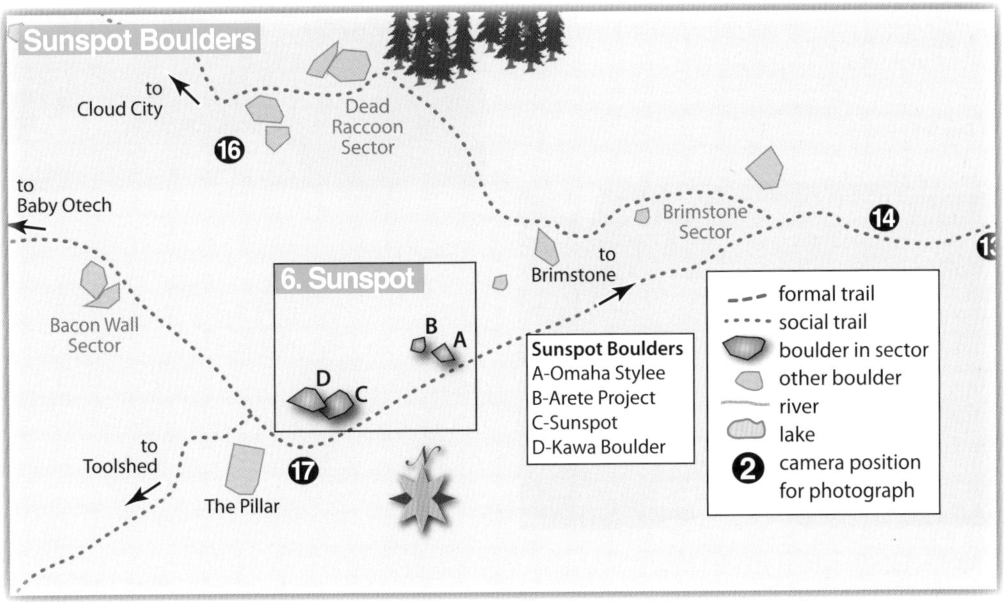

A. Omaha Stylee Boulder

This boulder has a small roof and lies just off the right side of the social trail, 20 yds from the short rock slabs.

❒ 1. **Omaha Stylee V11** ★
Start on a positive right-hand sidepull, the lower of the two, and a low left-hand flat edge. A hard move left, then straight up the short roof.
FA Harry Robertson 2003

❒ 2. **McFly V10** ★
Stand sitting, left hand on a crimp, right hand on a sloping edge. Move left, then up the face.
FA Wade David 2004

❒ 3. **V4** ★
Start sitting low and right and traverse the lip.

Omaha Stylee Boulder

B. Arête Project

❒ 1. **Arête Project**
Climb the white arête on the right side of the boulder.

Arête Project

C. Sunspot Boulder

A nice overhang that affords great views down to Lake Haiyaha. Continue uphill on the social trail 50 yds beyond Omaha Stylee. Sunspot is on the right.

❒ 1. **Sunspot V10** ★★
Start sitting, matched on a low jug. Climb straight out the overhang, through slopers and underclings to a committing move to the finish jug. Awesome climbing and setting. A Park classic.
FA David Graham 2001

❒ 2. **Sunspot Left V8**
Climb Sunspot to a large sloping rail, then head immediately left on edges.

❒ 3. **Minor Threat V3** ★
Start standing, on top of a boulder, on two adjacent crimps and climb crisp edges.

Sunspot Boulder

D. Kawa Boulder

This boulder sits on top of Sunspot Boulder.

❒ 1. **Kawa V10** ★
Start squatting on a left-hand sidepull and a right-hand sloper in the white rock. Climb up and then follow the seam left, eventually heading straight up the middle of the wall.
FA Ben Safdi 2005

Kawa Boulder

Approach Photo...more Upper Chaos

To approach the rest of the bouldering in Upper Chaos, continue on the social trail past Sunspot to The Pillar. The Pillar is a nice landmark that serves as the gateway to Upper Chaos. From here there is no trail and the only option is to pick your way over the talus. Head around the right side of The Pillar, over several sturdy roots. The enormous talus field will open up before you.

To access Baby Otech Sector, Gepetto's Workshop, Upper Chaos, Mirkwood Sector, and Eternia Sector, head straight into the talus, following directions to Top Notch Sector, which is the next sector covered in the book. To access Blood Money, Tool Shed Sector, and Upper Upper Chaos, head left, and follow directions to Tool Shed Sector. Cloud City and Jade are best initially approached from the Bacon Wall Secor, via Dead Raccoon and Brimstone. Once you've spent some time learning the lay of the land, Cloud City can be approached from Baby Otech Sector as well.

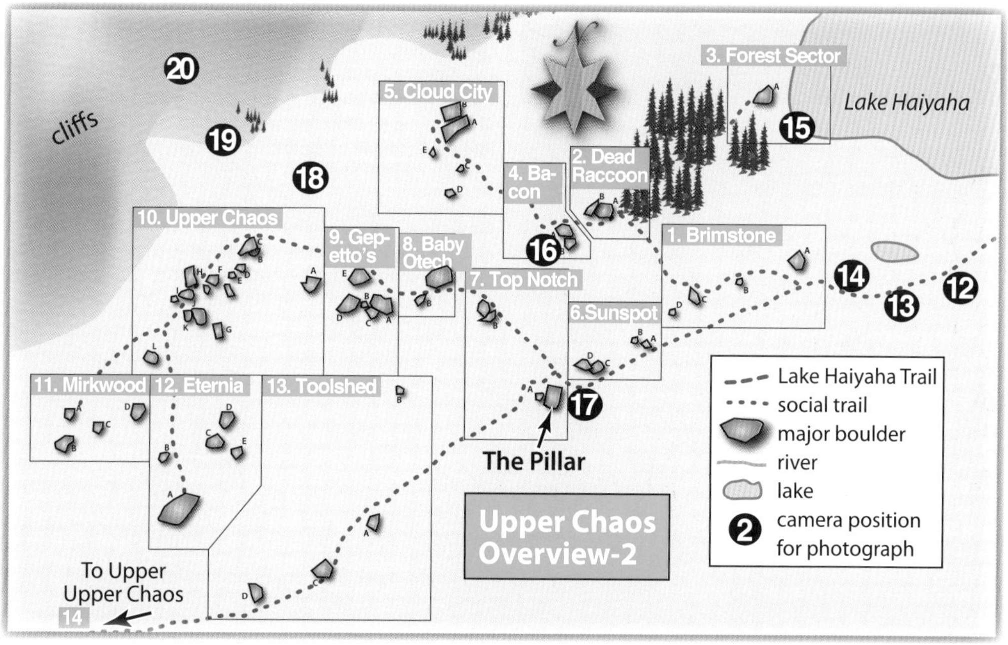

Tyler Landman

The seclusion and the seemingly endless amount of quality rock in Rocky Mountain National Park and Mt. Evans set them apart from some of the world's other, more renowned bouldering spots. The long and aggressive hikes, though rough at first, become a gratifying routine that prepares you for the day ahead rather than tiring you out, and on the way down, allows you the time to process and relax. There is a decidedly different feeling you get, being in such a remote and unspoiled place that truly feels wild and organic. The areas are relatively "young" in the broad spectrum of the history of climbing, which not only allows more opportunity to appreciate the area but also contribute to it, at every grade.

Tyler and Jeffery Landman have spent a number of years enjoying the gorgeous bouldering in RMNP. Photo: Landman Collection

Though I've had many memorable moments climbing in the Park and at Mt. Evans, some of my most unforgettable experiences took place on days I did not put on my climbing shoes. They were days I just spotted, the hikes that deviated from the trail and took me to untouched boulders that would grow to be personal favorites. Lightning storms spent hiding out in caves and being the last car left in the parking lot. Desolate early-season days walking over the top-outs of snow-covered boulders that would become so challenging to climb, and snowy late season evenings calling mother nature's bluff. But, most of all, returning after winter days training in the gym, and nights dreaming of revenge, to wrap up projects that were once out of reach.

Boulder, with its seemingly limitless amount of rock, draws climbers from all over the world. The climbing scene, both talented and motivated, make the area a hard place to justify leaving. With so much rock to test yourself on, and so many climbers to train with, this "environment" has raised the bar for achievement. This improvement ultimately returns to these areas that spawned it in the form of new first ascents and new standards, helping them to progress and develop.

Over the last 15 years climbing, I have learned that there is no better feeling than returning to the car, ravaged and sore after a long day out. That moment that earlier in the day seemed like it was a lifetime away from actually occurring. But after the last six years in the park, it has become clear that sometimes this feeling is better when you don't finish your project. It allows you to formulate your next return, even before you have left the parking lot. This is a testament to the area, a place that occupies your mind when you're gone, a place that is only maturing and getting better every year.

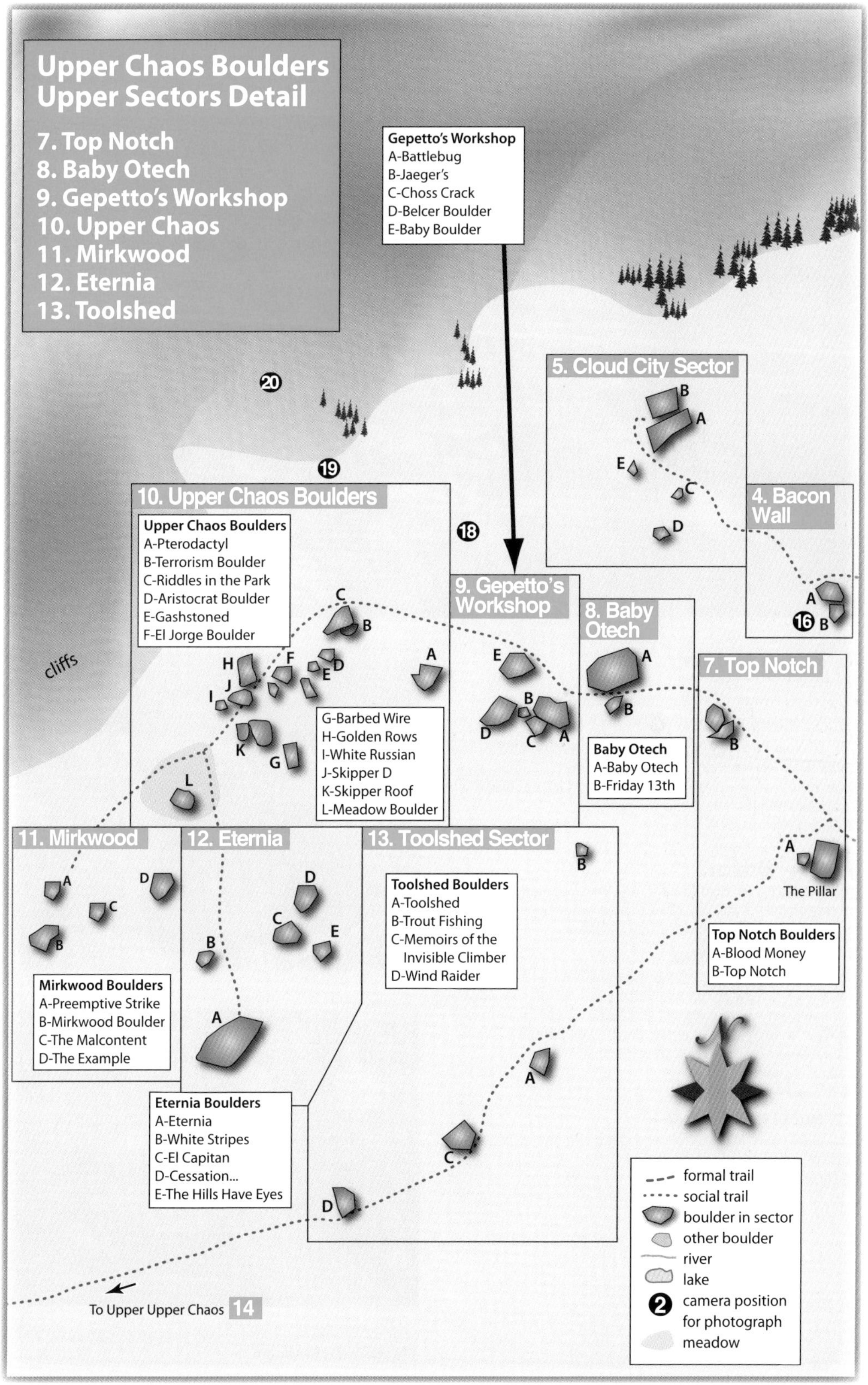
Upper Chaos Boulders
Upper Sectors Detail
7. Top Notch
8. Baby Otech
9. Gepetto's Workshop
10. Upper Chaos
11. Mirkwood
12. Eternia
13. Toolshed
Gepetto's Workshop
A-Battlebug
B-Jaeger's
C-Choss Crack
D-Belcer Boulder
E-Baby Boulder
5. Cloud City Sector
4. Bacon Wall
10. Upper Chaos Boulders
Upper Chaos Boulders
A-Pterodactyl
B-Terrorism Boulder
C-Riddles in the Park
D-Aristocrat Boulder
E-Gashstoned
F-El Jorge Boulder
G-Barbed Wire
H-Golden Rows
I-White Russian
J-Skipper D
K-Skipper Roof
L-Meadow Boulder
cliffs
9. Gepetto's Workshop
8. Baby Otech
Baby Otech
A-Baby Otech
B-Friday 13th
7. Top Notch
The Pillar
Top Notch Boulders
A-Blood Money
B-Top Notch
11. Mirkwood
Mirkwood Boulders
A-Preemptive Strike
B-Mirkwood Boulder
C-The Malcontent
D-The Example
12. Eternia
Eternia Boulders
A-Eternia
B-White Stripes
C-El Capitan
D-Cessation...
E-The Hills Have Eyes
13. Toolshed Sector
Toolshed Boulders
A-Toolshed
B-Trout Fishing
C-Memoirs of the Invisible Climber
D-Wind Raider
To Upper Upper Chaos 14
formal trail
social trail
boulder in sector
other boulder
river
lake
camera position for photograph
meadow

Top Notch Sector

This small zone lies in the middle of the talus field. Continue up to The Pillar, heading around the right side, stepping over some tree branches. Blood Money is 30 yds upcanyon from The Pillar and it faces the talus field (north). To get to Top Notch from Blood Money, head 75 yds north into the talus field.

A. Blood Money

Tucked behind a cluster of boulders, this steep roof is 30 yds upcanyon from The Pillar. The problem is obvious when viewed from the middle of the talus field. Faces the talus field.

❒ 1. **Blood Money V12** ★★
Start sitting, left hand on a sidepull and a right hand on a sloper on the arête. Climb the compression feature, taking care not to dab on the rock to the right.
FA Daniel Woods 2008

B. Top Notch

From Blood Money, hike straight into the talus field about 75 yds, heading for a small cluster of three larger boulders. This roof is somewhat hidden. Faces Lake Haiyaha.

❒ 1. **Top Notch V13** ★★★
Start sitting, right hand on an undercling, left hand on a flat sidepull. Climb straight up the wall on wonderfully flat edges, culminating in a hard jump move to a jug. Ty Landman made the FA in an impressive one-day effort. The first move is one of the hardest in the Park. A classic problem. Faces east, towards the lake.
FA Ty Landman 2008

❒ 2. **Hume Problem V7** ★
Start matched on a large hold and climb straight up on small holds over the lip.
FA Dave Hume 2009

Daniel Woods sends the classic overhang Top Notch V13. Photo by Steve Woods

Baby Otech Sector

The main attraction of the Baby Otech Sector is the Baby Otech Boulder — an important landmark in the sea of talus that is Upper Chaos. From the Pillar pick your way across the talus, diagonaling across the rocks, following the approach to Top Notch. From Top Notch, head 50 yds upcanyon and right, to a large basin. From the Bacon Wall Sector, head upcanyon, away from the lake; the Otech Boulder is about 100 yds away.

A. Baby Otech Boulder

A large boulder, and important landmark, somewhat set apart from the others.

❒ 1. **Baby Otech V10** ★★
Start standing, matched on a big jug on the arête, and traverse left through flat edges about 15 ft. Head straight up the wall.
FA David Graham 2005

❒ 2. **Otech Direct V9** ★
Start on edges and climb straight up into Baby Otech.
FA David Graham 2005

B. Friday the 13th Boulder

This short boulder sits just upcanyon and in front of Baby Otech. It faces uphill.

❒ 1. **Friday the 13th V10** ★
Start sitting on a small right-hand crimp and a left-hand undercling. Reach up left to a small crimp and dyno to the rounded jug. The first ascent was flashed.
FA Tyler Landman 2007

❒ 2. **Death Proof V5** ★
Start sitting and make a few powerful moves out right.

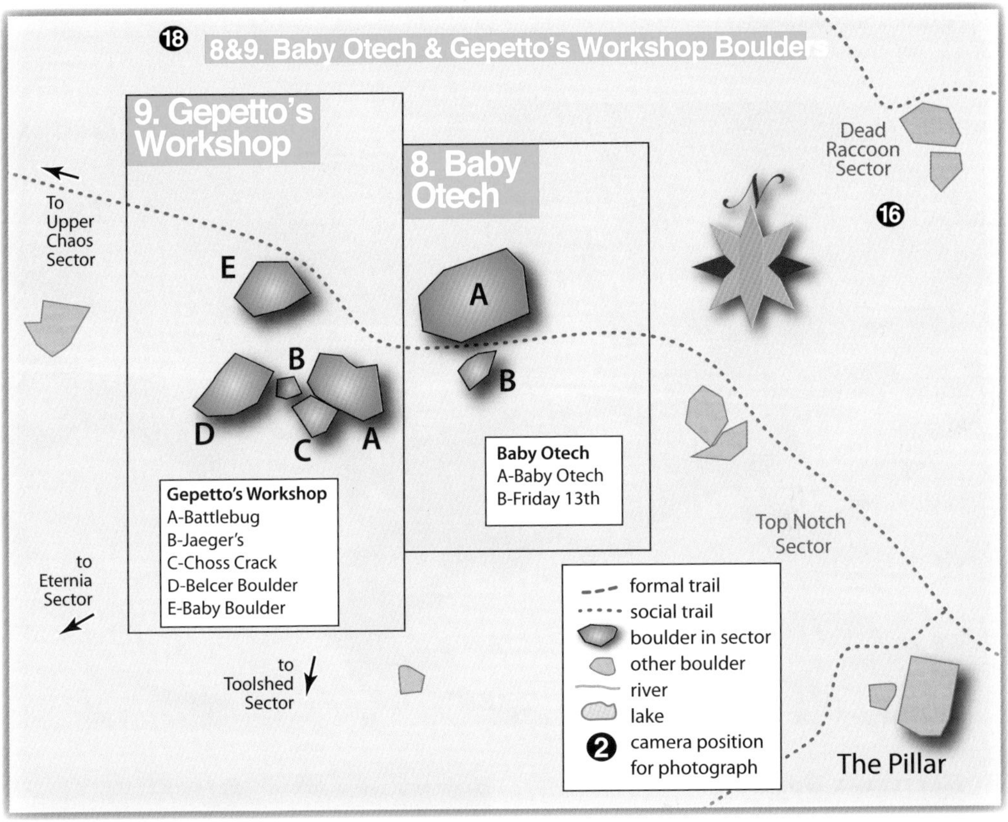
18
8&9. Baby Otech & Gepetto's Workshop Boulders
9. Gepetto's Workshop
8. Baby Otech
To Upper Chaos Sector
Dead Raccoon Sector
16
N
E
A
B
B
D
C
A
B
Baby Otech
A-Baby Otech
B-Friday 13th
Gepetto's Workshop
A-Battlebug
B-Jaeger's
C-Choss Crack
D-Belcer Boulder
E-Baby Boulder
to Eternia Sector
Top Notch Sector
to Toolshed Sector
formal trail
social trail
boulder in sector
other boulder
river
lake
2 camera position for photograph
The Pillar

Gepetto's Workshop

Just uphill from Friday the 13th. Head up to a small boulderless patch of tundra. Gepetto's Workshop Sector is just uphill on the left.

A. Battlebug Boulder

The first large boulder on the left, just beyond a small patch of grass and dirt.

❒ 1. **Battlebug V7** ★
Start matched on a large sloper and climb straight up on good edges to a tricky mantel.

❒ 2. **Battlebug Traverse V8** ★
Start matched on a large sloper and head right on rough edges to a good hold.
FA Chuck Fryberger 2009

❒ 3. **Not Bacon Wall V5** ★
Walk right of the Battlebug Traverse 15 ft. Sit start and climb straight up the wall.

B. Hate B Boulder

Just around the corner from Battlebug is Not Bacon Wall, and to the right, down in a large hole, is the Hate B Boulder.

❒ 1. **Hate B V8**
Climb up the face, starting on a left-hand gaston and a right-hand edge. Make a hard move to the pinch, avoiding the arête. A silly contrivance.
FA Justin Jaeger 2009

C. Choss Crack

❒ 1. **Choss Crack V3**
Climb the crack to a tricky and scary finish.

D. Belcer's Boulder

Travesse is hidden uphill from Not Bacon Wall. Facing Not Bacon Wall, turn around and scramble up the slab to the left. Travesse appears down to the left, at the top of the boulder.

❒ 1. **Travesse V7** ★★
Sit down start. Following the right-to-left line of upward rising edges to a crux pull at the lip.
FA Jim Belcer 2002

E. Baby Boulder

From the Not Bacon Wall, head upcanyon 15 yds to this overhanging boulder.

❒ 1. **Project**
Climb the arête from a low start.

❒ 2. **Paul's Problem V3** ★★
Start on good edges, climb up and right.
FA Paul Otis 2002

Hate B Boulder

Belcer's Boulder

Baby Boulder

Choss Crack

Upper Chaos

Upper Chaos is home to some of the most classic boulders in the Park. This area has steep, hard problems, incredible scenery, and excellent rock quality. From the Baby Boulder continue along the middle of the ridge to a small opening, just left of a cluster of trees. Pterodactyl will appear on your left.

A. Pterodactyl Boulder

This massive boulder has a couple of classic problems. From the Not Bacon Wall, hike upcanyon 50 yds, staying uphill from the bottom of the drainage on your right. Hike around the right side of a large boulder to a narrow point with a spiked rock. The problem is on the left.

❒ 1. **Pterodactyl V12** ★★★
Start sitting on small sloping edge. Move the left hand up first, then follow a nice line of edges into the stand start. Finish up the dihedral feature.
FA Andre DiFelice 2008

❒ 2. **Pterodactyl Stand V9** ★★★
Start standing, matched on a low sloping rail, and climb up the dihedral.
FA Jamie Emerson 2008

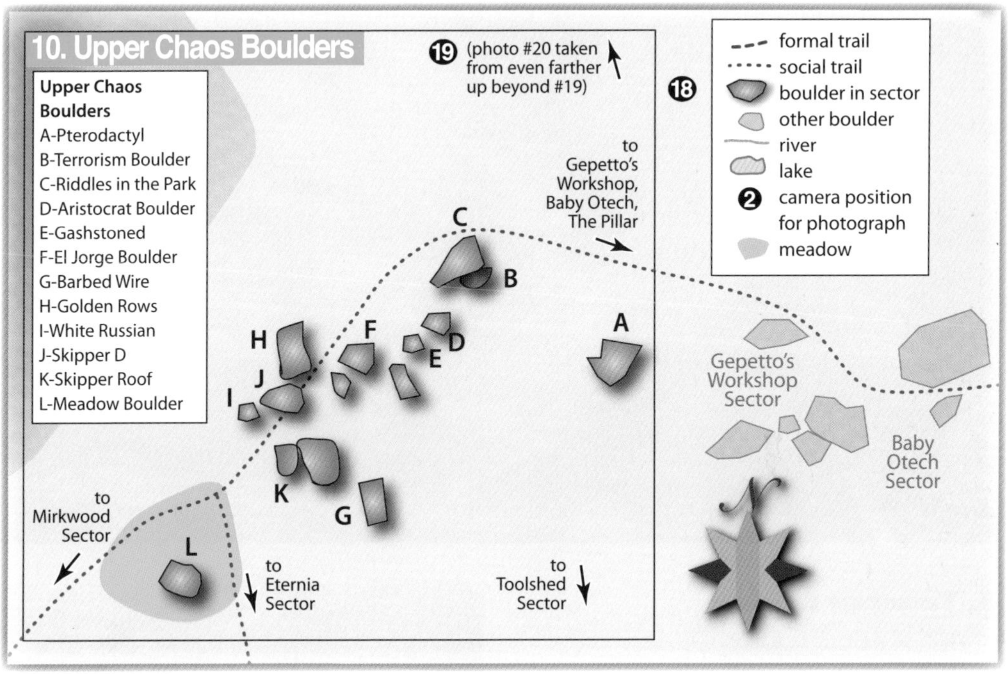

An evening storm shrouds the mountains in fog. Photo by Caroline Treadway

Terrorism Boulder and Riddles in the Park Boulder

B. Terrorism Boulder

One hundred yards down from Pterodactyl at the bottom of a small basin, these two large boulders will come into view.

❒ 1. **Terrorism Arête V7** ★★

Start standing on good holds at the base of the arête. Climb straight up and slightly left at the top. Terrifying late in the season with no snow, casual earlier in the year.

FA David Graham 2001

C. Riddles in the Park Boulder

❒ 1. **The Hobbit V12** ★★

Start right hand on a flat edge undercling underneath the roof and left hand on a flat edge at the lip. Make a move to a weird and sharp left-hand edge, grab a counterpart edge for the right. A huge lockoff follows. The landing is much better early in the summer.

FA Jamie Emerson 2008

❒ 2. **The Hobbit Stand V10** ★★

Start on two sharp crimps at the lip of the roof. A hard lockoff.

FA Jamie Emerson 2008

❒ 3. **Riddles in the Dark V10** ★★★

Start matched on a triangular undercling and climb out the roof. The first ascent was done early in the season, and as the snow melted the lower holds for Riddles in the Park were revealed. The snow melts so much that it is difficult to start this problem late in the year.

FA Jamie Emerson 2006

❒ 4. **Riddles in the Park V12** ★★★

Start low in the overhang on an incut right hand and an edge for the left. Climb several moves into the start of Riddles in the Dark Awesome steep climbing.

FA Paul Robinson 2006

Riddles in the Park- Whirlwind

❒ 5. **Vortex V8**

Stand start on a sharp left-hand gaston and right hand on a sharp hold on the arête. Climb up and left.

FA David Graham 2005

❒ 6. **Whirlwind V6**

Around the right from Riddles in the Park. Start sitting matched on bad undercling holds in the dihedral. A tricky bit of beta will get you off the ground. Ryan Olson nearly did the first ascent, but was called off route by a spotter who jokingly called "dab." Olson nobly stepped aside.

FA Jamie Emerson 2006

hoto and Design: Gustavo Moser. www.Gas-Photo.com

D. Aristocrat Boulder

Hike right, around Riddles in the Park. Aristocrat is 10 yds beyond the end of Riddles, on the left.

❒ 1. **Aristocrat V9** ★★
Start sitting on a left-hand edge and a right-hand undercling. Climb straight up, making a hard move off a right-hand undercling.
FA Jeff Landman 2007

E. Gashstoned Boulder

To reach this somewhat hidden problem, walk uphill from Aristocrat and slightly right for five yards; then crawl down into a hole.

❒ 1. **Gashstoned V5** ★
Start in the bottom of the hole and climb straight up. Scary.
FA Chad Greedy 2006

Aristocrat Boulder

Gashstoned Boulder

Tyler Landman on Terrorism Arête V7.
Photo by Caroline Treadway

F. El Jorge Boulder

Continue in the faint and jumbled wash for 25 yds past Riddles in the Park. This overhang is obscured until the last minute, but it faces the trail on the left.

❒ 1. **The Core V8** ★★
Start matched on a flat jug at the base of the overhang. Climb up, then left. Originally named "The Core," but many refer to this as Far Left El Jorge.
FA Scott Hahn 2003

❒ 2. **Left El Jorge V11** ★★★
Start matched on a flat jug at the base of the overhang. Climb straight up the wall, using several intermediates to reach a sloping hold in a seam for the left hand. Top out. Classic Park climbing. Hard.
FA David Graham 2001

❒ 3. **Right El Jorge V8** ★★
Start matched on a flat jug at the base of the overhang. Climb up and right, moving through a razor sharp crimp and a huge lockoff to sloping rail feature for the right hand.
FA David Graham 2001

G. Barbed Wire Beard Boulder

Barbed Wire Beard is 10 yards uphill from Left Jorge. Walk around the left side of Left El Jorge and head up into the talus, staying left of a deep pit.

❒ 1. **Fuzzy Wuzzy V8** ★
Start on the right side, climb up and right, out of the hole.

❒ 2. **Barbed Wire Beard V11** ★★
Start standing at the right side of the wall, matched on an edge at about 5 ft. Cross over right hand and traverse the amazing flat edges from right to left, to a hard sequence at the end.
FA Adam Osterhoff 2003

❒ 3. **Barbed Wire Moustache V11** ★
Start squatting with hands very wide, left hand on a sidepull, right hand on a sidpull. Make a hard move to a good edge for the right hand and climb straight up into the crux of Barbed Wire Beard.
FA David Graham 2003

H. Golden Rows of Flows

From Left El Jorge, walk right 7 yds.

❒ 1. **Golden Rows of Flows V11** ★★
Start right hand on a sloping undercling, left hand on a small sidepull 5 ft to the left. Climb straight up on miserable crimps.
FA David Graham 2001
Note: Many now start matched on the undercling, by stepping off the ground. This is V10. Stepping off the rock, starting matched on the undercling is V9.

I. White Russian

Walk around Golden Rows of Flows to the left. 5yds beyond the boulder, down and slightly left are these two small problems.

❒ 1. **White Russian V9**
Start matched on a good hold, down in the hole, climb up and left. Hard not to dab. Looks much better than it climbs.
FA Simon Moore 2007

❒ 2. **Arête V5** ★
Start matched on a sloping pinch. Climb up and right.

Jackie Moore on Right El Jorge V8. Photo by Caroline Treadway

J. Skipper D Boulder

Walk around Golden Rows of Flows to the left. Skipper D is 10 yds beyond, on the left.

❒ 1. **Skipper D V8** ★★★
Start standing matched in a rounded jug. Climb straight up through pinches and sidepulls. One of the best of the grade in the Park.
FA David Graham 2001

❒ 2. **Skipping on the Roof V9** ★
The wall opposite Skipper Roof holds a tall and difficult problem. Start on an obvious jug, and climb up through the hole. Scary.
FA Tyler Landman 2007

K. Skipper Roof

This boulder is adjacent to Skipper D on the right. Walk to the start of Skipper D and then down and right to the cave.

❒ 1. **Skipper Right V10** ★★
Start on a right-hand flat undercling and a left-hand sloping edge. Climb out the overhanging feature, directly to a sharp arête hold. Top out to the right.
FA David Graham 2001

❒ 2. **Skipper Left V11** ★★
Start as for Skipper Right and head left after the first move. Good tension climbing leads to a hard move to a flat gaston. Top out straight up, through the hole.
FA David Graham 2001

❒ 3. **Next Friday V11** ★
Start on a good left-hand undercling and an edge. Set a right heel and make a long move, climbing into the top of Skipper Left. Top out through the hole.
FA Ty Landman 2007

Courtney Greedy and Amanda Woods bouldering on Meadow Boulder. Photo by Steve Woods

L. Meadow Boulder

The Meadow Boulder sits in an absolutely gorgeous setting above the tree line, high in the Park. A good place to warm up if you're climbing in Upper Chaos. Hallett Peak looms above. The Meadow is about 2.5 miles from the trailhead.

❒ 1. **Chad's Bulge V3** ★
Hard.
FA Chad Greedy 2001

❒ 2. **V1** ★
Start on Chad's Bulge, head left.

❒ 3. **V2** ★
Start on incuts, climb to a long move off a right-facing gaston. There are more easy warm-ups on the right side of the face.

Meadow Boulder

Mirkwood Sector

From the Meadow Boulder, hike 50 yds or so up into the talus, up a snowy gully at the base of a broken cliff on the right. Preemptive Strike is on a distinctive white boulder, 25 yds below Mirkwood.

A. Preemptive Strike

❒ 1. **Preemptive Strike V8** ★★
Start with a right hand on the arête, left hand on a sidepull. Climb the compression feature. This has yet to be climbed starting matched on the left-hand sidepull, as an undercling.
FA Justin Jaeger 2009

B. Mirkwood Boulder

❒ 1. **Mirkwood V10** ★★
Start standing on a good left-hand edge and a small right-hand gaston crimper. Tension filled climbing leads out the overhang.
FA Jamie Emerson 2009

❒ 2. **I Comb My Hair Like God (aka Mirkwood sit) V11** ★★★
Start crouched on two opposing sidepulls and a toe hook out right. Nice flat edges. A couple of hard moves lead into Mirkwood.
FA Phil Schaal 2009

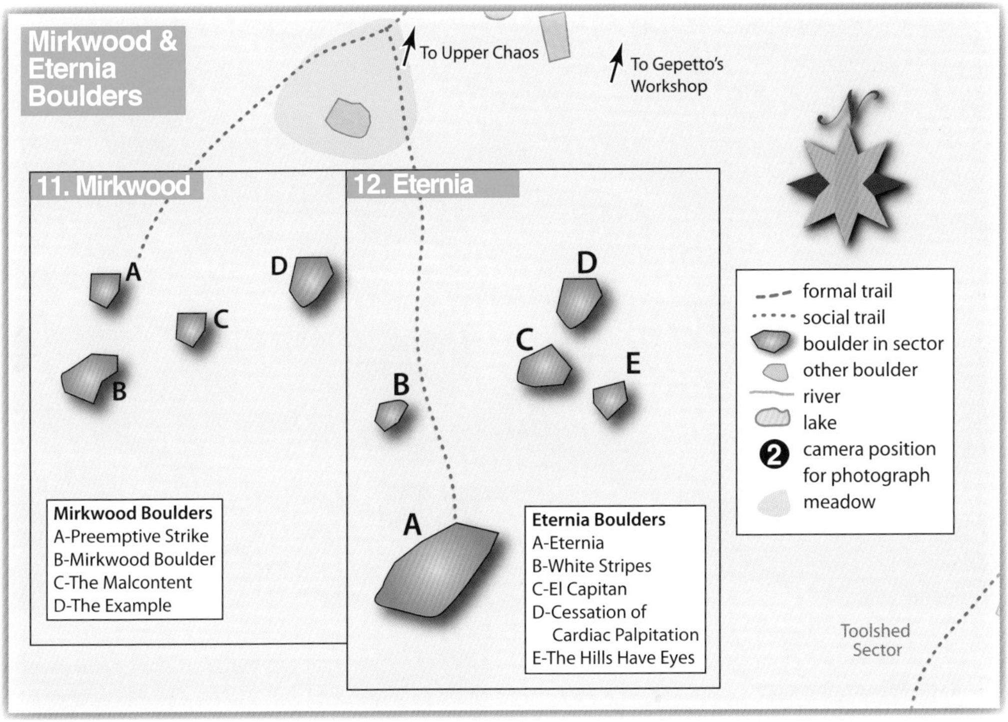

Brian Camp powers his way through Skipper Right V11. Photo by Ryan Olson

C. The Malcontent

Straight down the hill from Mirkwood — 10 yds away.

❒ 1. **Chaos Edges V3** ★★

Start sitting and climb the awesome incuts.

❒ 2. **The Malcontent V7** ★

Start sitting, low, on the right side of the face, on a right hand incut and a left-hand sloper pinch. Traverse left, then head up.

FA Justin Jaeger 2009

D. The Example

Downhill from Mirkwood 30 yds. Faces upcanyon.

❒ 1. **The Example V2** ★★★

Start on a good edge and climb the striking face. Classic.

FA Ryan Silven 2009

The Malcontent

The Example

A Cure for the Common Darkness:

Justin Jaeger

I spent way too many hours of my wakeful prepubescent life staring at catalogues and magazines that preached the sweet promises of the Great American Outdoors. Adventures of every variety seemed to be out there, waiting. But as time wore on I noticed that the synapses most burnt and dredged through my otherwise listless and negligently un-medicated mind led to those amazing areas of our fair land that are kissed by radiant sunshine, whipped by powerful winds, and tickled by the clearest waters. Places where a man could sit on the spongy earth, damp with the dew of the evening, and still be a mile closer to the starlit heavens above than any tortured soul in the cities below. Places where a man can let a raging thunderhead pressure-wash away his darkness. Places where a man can let his wounds bleed dry.

After so many dead ends and broken promises of a life more worth living, I found myself amidst the Rocky Mountains of Colorado. Though just barely beyond the clinking cacophony of trekking poles, the constant zipping and unzipping of quick-dry convertible pants, and meaningless small talk of the deluded masses, I found myself awestruck in the glorious quasi-backcountry of Rocky Mountain National Park. The tight grain of the stone and gentle rise and morning surface slurp of the trout made me feel an immediate ease. The life of the area could be heard in every drip from melting snow and ice, felt in each calming whoosh of the breeze through the pines, and smelled in the overwhelming organic freshness that seemed to permeate every nook and cranny. It seemed and felt right in a way more profound than the hipster mountain-wear marketing robber barons could explain, and certainly more so than I can hope to impress upon you now.

Since those first experiences, the years marched on to bring an exponential multiplication of humans who now scurry about the blocks in plentitude like cockroaches in Gotham. But even now the wildness cannot be ignored. Vestiges of it abound. Gnarled and gale-twisted pines stab into the clear blue skies like mangled old fingers flipping the bird to their bitter foe. Deep scars cut across titanic stone faces as a grim reminder of the cataclysmic collisions that sparked their life and death. Haggard but resilient elk walk proudly and casually about the place with a look in their eye that taking your life wouldn't mean a damn thing. Even the swirled patterns trapped in the stone hint of their creation from a brooding, churning, primordial witches stew. And so it was, I quickly discovered that everything in the alpine has a double life — a radiant shine and a dismal darkness. The talus blocks that can strike terror into one's heart with the slightest hint of airborne moisture also provide shelter from the raging winds and pelting hailstones of the inevitable alpine storms. The sculpted, angular edges can give purchase to the most desperate of climbing attempts or can rip and ravage your last layer of skin. Dynamic movements even slightly above the jagged landings give a sense of desperation and commitment normally reserved for the stratospheric. And of course, the feeling of tourist-induced claustrophobia and the misery of parking wars in one instant can pass and yield to the most intimate moments of an untamed wilderness in another. Just out back, not too far away, the haunting nothingness fills you with everything.

Our little game has a double life here as well. One of discovery and self discovery. Where small enclaves can be found amongst the stone for the self to flourish amongst friends and rise to great heights, yet remain hidden from the writhing misery of the outside world. Where terror and companionship can cultivate the deepest satisfaction of belonging to something less bastardized by finance and the race of rats. But the alpine is also a grand stage where egos can boom through the canyons in rapture or agony like rolling thunder from an approaching storm. Where pawns in our little world can carve out their relevance with inspired efforts. Where the outcast can be reborn to a new tribe to carry on its traditions, miracles, and sins.

In the jagged blocks of talus, there is life and death. The alpha and the omega. Creation and destruction for as wide as the eye can see and the soul can wander.

And after all the transient human drama, sweat, and blood is washed from the stone at the end of our pathetic comedy and the evening's chill blankets the valley, you cannot help but realize that what really lasts is the savage nobility of the place. It creeps into everyone who spends any amount of time here. It cannot be helped. It is the way and it's bigger than any one of us. We can only hope to become a part of its history, its story, and hang on as long as we can to something eternal and true.

Eternia Sector

Eternia Sector sits atop of a large pile of boulders, overlooking the meadow. From the Meadow Boulder, head up the talus for 150 yds to a large roof, which faces the meadow. There are other good problems along the way.

A. Eternia

❒ 1. **Eternia V11** ★★★
Start in the far back of the cave, sitting, matched on a large sloping feature. Climb straight out the very steep and long roof. The power endurance testpiece of the Park. Dave famously challenged climbers to "hike up there and tell me how hard it is." Classic. Eternia is at an elevation of 10,511 ft.
FA Dave Graham 2001

❒ 2. **Reternia V11** ★★★
Start standing, facing out the roof, matched on an undercling. Follow the seam and finish on Eternia. Matt Tschol started sitting on the rock, and calls his slightly lower start "Retardia V9."
FA Daniel Woods 2006

Eternia

B. The White Stripes

At the bottom of the hill below Eternia. Faces up towards Eternia.

❒ 1. **The White Stripes V9** ★★
Sit start with a left-hand sidepull and climb straight up through a hard right-shoulder move. Moving out right is V6.
FA Mike Auldridge 2003

The White Stripes

C. El Capitan Boulder

On the hillside below Eternia. This massive boulder faces the meadow.

❒ 1. **Mimicking Victory V9** ★★
Start standing, left hand on a pinch, right hand on a low flat undercling. Make a hard move to a flat, V-shaped hold. Climb straight up.
FA Adam Osterhoff 2003

❒ 2. **El Capitan V7** ★★★
This is a classic face and is quite an adventure—depending upon how much the snow has melted. The upper section is V2 and the grade goes up the lower one starts.

El Capitan Boulder

D. Cessation of Cardiac Palpitation Boulder

In the small basin to the left of and below El Capitan Boulder is a large boulder with one problem. Cessation faces back towards Meadow Boulder.

❒ 1. **Cessation of Cardiac Palpitation V11** ★★
Starts low on edges at the bottom of the hole. Climb up and left on nice flat edges. Finishes straight up the black face on gaston crimps.
FA Blake Rutherford 2005

E. The Hills Have Eyes Boulder

❒ 1. **The Hills Have Eyes V4** ★★★
Stand start and climb up the middle of the face.
FA Chad Greedy 2003

The Hills Have Eyes

Cessation of Cardiac Palpitation

Toolshed Sector

The best way to approach Toolshed Sector is to hike straight upcanyon from The Pillar, staying on the left (south) side of the boulderfield. Look for Chaotic Glacier, heading straight over the talus toward this obvious landmark. About 100 yds from The Pillar is Toolshed Boulder, which faces upcanyon.

Toolshed Sector

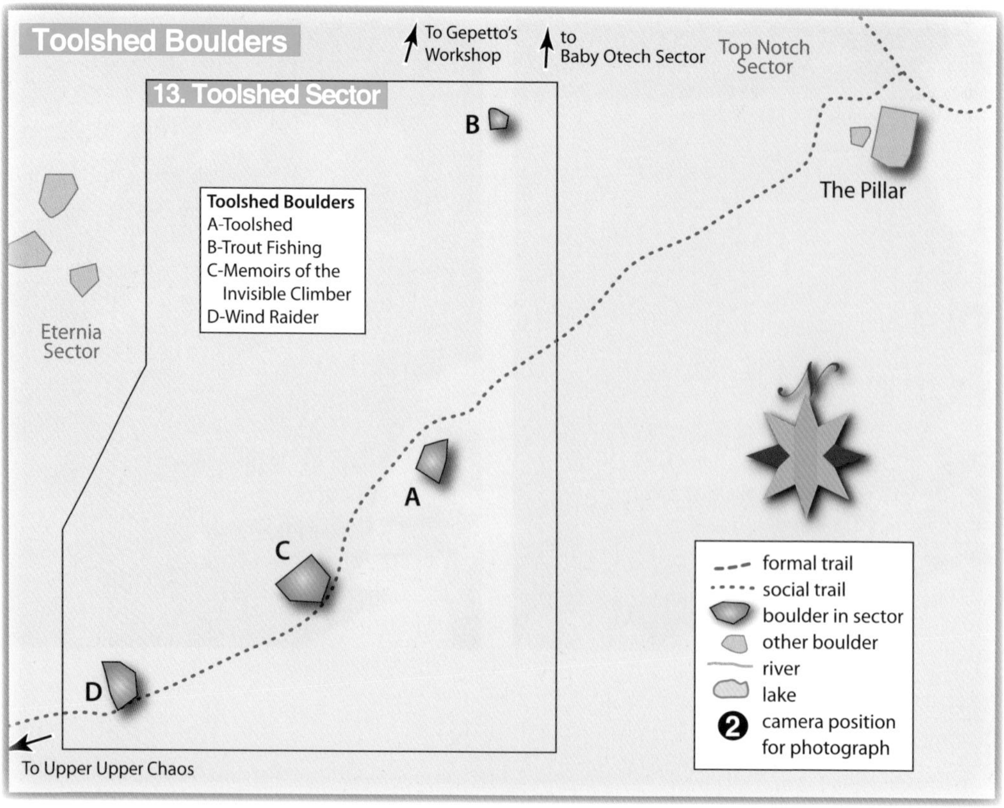

A. Toolshed Boulder

❒ 1. **Toolshed Right V7** ★
Start on a sharp slot for the left hand, and a lower, flat, right-hand sidepull. Move right and top out up sharp jugs.
FA Paul Otis 2002

❒ 2. **Toolshed Left V8** ★
Start on a sharp slot for the left hand, and a lower, flat, right-hand sidepull. Move up and left, climbing up the faint dihedral on rough rock.
FA Paul Otis 2002

❒ 3. **Sinister Secret V10** ★★
Start squatting on a right-hand sidepull and a low left-hand crimp. Stab to the left-hand slot, and finish on Toolshed Left.
FA Justin Jaeger 2008

❒ 4. **The Ecstatic Truth V10** ★
Start as for Sinister Secret, but head right at the slot, finishing on Toolshed Right.
FA Jamie Emerson 2008

B. Trout Fishing Boulder

Facing the Toolshed Boulder, head left 75 yds over the talus towards a small hill covered in trees and a small dark overhang. An isolated problem, but worth the effort. Baby Otech is 30 yds beyond the Trout Fishing in the same direction.

❒ 1. **Trout Fishing in America V1** ★★★
Start matched on a good, left-facing edge. Climb up edges to the top. Classic.
FA Jamie Emerson 2010

C. Memoirs of the Invisible Climber Boulder

❒ 1. **Memoirs of the Invisible Climber V12** ★★★
Start sitting at the base of the dihedral on a good, sloping hold. Climb up the prow right of the dihedral. Finish out right. Was originally V9, but a broken hold has bumped up the difficulty to V12.
FA Chris Sharma 2001
FA after break Jon Glassberg 2010

Toolshed Boulder

Trout Fishing in America

Memoirs of the Invisible Climber

Trout Fishing in America Approach

C. Wind Raider Boulder

Continue upcanyon 100 yds from Memoirs of the Invisible Climber. Head left of a huge boulder which is fractured and sunk into the talus. the Wind Raider Boulder is just beyond this landmark, on the left. It faces uphill.

❒ 1. **Wind Raider V10** ★★
On the left side of the face. Start on two crimps and climb straight up. The arête is not usable from the starting holds.
FA Blake Rutherford 2007

❒ 2. **Face Full of Mez V9** ★★★
Start matched on a jug in the middle of the wall. Climb straight up the face.
FA Luke Parady 2003

Wind Raider Boulder

Jon Glassberg on his problem Easy on the Eyes V9. Photo by Greg Mionski

Upper Upper Chaos

Above Eternia there are nearly endless boulders. There are hundreds of first ascents to be climbed and at the time of this writing, only a few brave souls have ventured this far. The following problems are mentioned for historical reference, and to hopefully encourage climbers to continue hiking. Jim Belcer, Paul Otis, David Graham and Jon Linhart were the first climbers to hike up here, in 2001, and they named the area Upper Upper Chaos. Paul established Full Chaos V10, and Jim Belcer added Mr. Hanky V9.

To get to Upper Upper Chaos, hike up the left side of the canyon beyond Wind Raider. A large basin of big boulders will open up on your right. There are still many projects to be climbed here. Continue steeply upcanyon to a large permanent snowfield. Hike up the snowfield for 200 yds, passing many boulders and potential new problems on your right. One of the newest additions is Never Never Land, a Jon Glassberg problem on the right, which faces the snowfield. Seventy-five yards beyond, near the top of the snow, is a cluster of boulders on the left, away from the main talus field. Full Chaos is in this cluster, somewhat hidden, and left, facing the steep, broken mountainside of Otis Peak. This problem is usually buried with snow until the end of June, and then becomes a dangerous endeavour as the snow melts. Continuing upcanyon there are literally hundreds of unclimbed boulders. Glassberg and Ryan Silven added a number of new problems in the summer of 2010, including Scoot's Roof (which sits atop the Ice Cave), The Outcast V11, Spinabifida V11, and Dodecahedral V10 and they referred to the area as Super Chaos. There are many unclimbed boulders in this sector, including the mentioned "Ice Cave" project, found by Jamie Emerson and Wade David in 2003. A great place to start looking is a small pond on the south side of Chaos Canyon. The black roof on the north shore is an outstanding new project for the next generation. The elevation of the pond is 10,987 ft.

❐ 1. **Never Never Land V11** ★★★
Start standing, on a left-hand sloping crimp and a small right-hand crimp. Climb up through a tricky sequence. An excellent addition in the summer of 2010.
FA Jon Glassberg 2010

❐ 2. **Easy on the Eyes V9** ★★★
Start standing on the ramp. A couple moves lead to a difficult jump.
FA Jon Glassberg 2010

❐ 3. **Full Chaos V10** ★★★★
Start sitting at the base of the overhang. Climb the faint dihedral, then head right on incut crimps. The line was named for its vague resemblance to the classic V10 in Hueco Tanks, Full Service. Early in the year this landing is very manageable; later in the year it is terrifying. A great problem, well worth the long hike. Elevation: 10,869 ft.
FA Paul Otis 2002
Blake Rutherford added some problems in 2005.

❐ 4. **Contents Under Pressure V9** ★★★
Blake's description of this problem is as follows: "It's 50-100 yds toward Hallett's from Full Chaos. If you are looking at the prominent spike, that is on that level, from below, the problem is 50 yds past and 50 yds left of a lichened face." This is a quality problem worth a mention and while difficult to find, is listed for historical purposes.
FA Blake Rutherford 2005

He also writes of a classic V5: "30 to 40 yds back towards the spike is a V5 in a slot that has exceptional rock and is over 20 ft. There is a long reach from a jug gaston to the lip. You can step off at any move but really can't fall. I've taken a few people there, and that one should be included."

Never Never Land

Easy on the Eyes

Full Chaos

Summer flowers in bloom in Upper Chaos Canyon

Alphabetical Index

Symbols

A

B

C

G

H

I

J

K

L

M

N

O

P

Q

R

S

T

U

V

Nymph Lake Photo by Caroline Treadway

Index by Grade

V15

V14

V13

V12

V12 (Cont'd)

V11

V10

V9

V8

V7

V6

V5

Lake Haiyaha

V4

V3

V2

V1

V0

Projects

513.b (random reference climb)

Sunset on Mt. Evans

About the Author
Jamie Emerson

Jamie Emerson was born in Toledo, Ohio and raised in Temperance, MI. He began climbing in college at Michigan State Unversity, toproping at the short sandstone cliff of Grand Ledge. In the following years, he developed a love for bouldering. Since then he has dedicated much of his life to the pursuit. He has traveled around the world, to South Africa, Switzerland, France, and all over the US and Canada following his passion for climbing, distilled and pure. In his free time, he runs B3bouldering.com, enjoys long hikes through desolate New Mexican canyons, reading Modern literature and epic poetry, and debating the finer points of grading ethics, philosophy, economics and political policy.

A HUGE THANKS
To Our Sponsors

Our sponsors are key to the sucess of this project. We whole-heartedly thank them and urge you to support them. They are core companies who love climbing and climbers.

FiveTen	Back Cover
Arc'Teryx	4
Black Diamond	13
Neptune Mountaineering	20
Organic Climbing	31
Metolius	85
Movement Climbing + Fitness	95
Nicros	133
Scarpa	141
Boulder Rock Club	156
Moon Climbing	165
Colorado Mountain School	175
Three Ball Climbing	180
The Spot	197

Sharp End Titles

By Kelly Sheridan

Central Washington Bouldering: Leavenworth & Gold Bar

Central Washington is jam-packed with quality granite boulders. From the endless folds of Leavenworth's forested canyons to the hilltop Shangri-la of Gold Bar, Washington offers something for everyone. Specific beta, detailed maps, and dozens of rich images will get you psyched.

By Darren Mabe

Clear Creek Canyon (CO)

Clear Creek Canyon is one of the primary destinations for Front Range sport climbers. This comprehensive and thorough guide is long overdue given the recent surge in route development. Local activist and route developer Darren Mabe brings his love and knowledge of the canyon to this full-color work.

By Bernard Gillett

Rock Climbing St Vrain Canyons (CO)

A renewed interest in this pristine area has uncovered hundreds of new and previously undocumented routes, suitable for climbers of all abilities. Come and enjoy one of the best-kept secrets of the Front Range: the St. Vrain Canyons offer a fresh and peaceful climbing experience, nestled in the foothills east of Rocky Mountain National Park.

Eldorado Canyon A Climbing Guide

Eldordo Canyon—with its red rock walls, cascading creek, and dazzling lichen—is the crown jewel of Colorado climbing. Intricate movement and cerebral climbing draw visitors from around the world. Adventure awaits on the multi-pitch outings and distant crags, while roadside routes greet the afterwork crowd. Few areas offer the ambiance and grand atmosphere of this magical venue.

Climbing Boulder's Flatirons

The Flatirons, forming the famed skyline above Boulder, are home to a plethora of classic lines. For the first time, a comprehensive full-color book will guide climbers to the hundreds of waiting adventures. Includes overview maps, photo-overlays, gear lists and GPS coordinates.

By Jason Haas

Fun Climbs Colorado

Looking for epic-free climbing outings suited for kids, visiting family and older climbers? Insightful advice attends to the special needs of climbing with family members of all ages. This guide also bridges the gap between climbing guide and vacation planner detailing logistical information necessary for families.

By Sibylle Hechtel

Fun Climbs Red Rocks (NV)

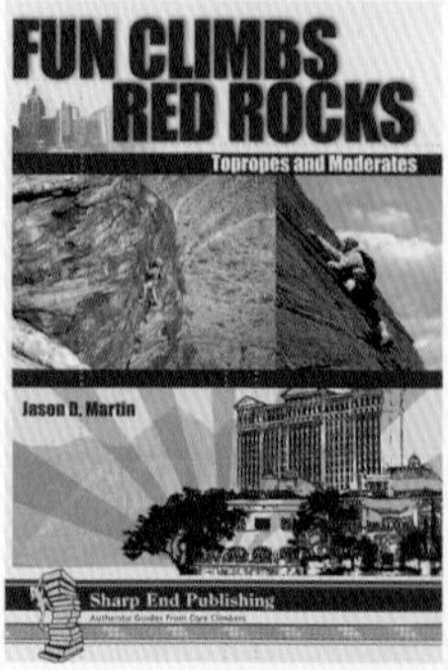

Las Vegas' Red Rocks is one of the premier climbing destinations in the US. This modern-era guide provides a detailed road map for the visiting climber looking for epic-free outings.

By Jason Martin

Order online at:
www.SharpEndBooks.com